Second Edition

RV Retirement
in the 21st Century

How to Live and Travel
in a Recreational Vehicle

by Jane Kenny

D1316000

Published by:

Roundabout Publications
PO Box 19235
Lenexa, KS 66285
Phone: 800-455-2207
Internet: www.TravelBooksUSA.com

Library of Congress Control Number: 2014935677

ISBN-10: 1-885464-52-5
ISBN-13: 978-1-885464-52-1

Acknowledgements

"…Two roads diverged in a wood, and I—
I took the one less traveled by,
And that has made all the difference."
— *Robert Frost*

The material in this book is drawn from the experiences of two senior citizens who decided to retire to RV travels. I am a novice to the camping/RV lifestyle compared to my husband Jack who has nearly four decades of experience as a camper and RVer. Retiring to an RV – for me – evolved into such a noteworthy experience that I decided to write a "how to" book about it.

Thank you, Jack, for urging me to "unretire" to do it, and for cheering me on through the long hours of tapping the keyboard. I could not have created this book without our RV pilot and my best friend…driver extraordinaire and resident RV technician.

Special thanks to Tim and David Cattelino of Roundabout Publications for their ongoing support, valued advice, professionalism and integrity. Your friendship is deeply appreciated!

Thank you to our many RV friends who furnished their own experiences and a lot of the information that came to be incorporated into the book. To all the dear people who love to go "on the road again," you're my heroes!

Finally, and as always, my deep gratitude goes out to my family – in particular my sons Walter and Warren – for their moral support and encouragement.

Jane

Dedicated To Granny's Darlings:
Nicholas, Peter, Collin, Katie, Dylan,
William, Benjamin, Annie, Megan and Ashlyn.
Always travelin' with me...in my heart.

Contents

Introduction

This book was written by a retiree in an RV.

RV Retirement has been compiled to share the knowledge, experience and skills we developed while spending our retirement years in an RV. The book is for RV "newbies" and for RV retirement "wannabies." If you are new to RVing or plan to use an RV when you retire, this is the book for you.

Retirement! It is the focus of books, magazines, newspaper articles, radio and TV interviews, seminars and more. Retirement is on the minds of working individuals for many years before they actually retire. How often during my working years did I hear, "When I retire, I'm going to…(you fill in the blanks)," from one of my co-workers? How often did I myself think, longingly, about my own retirement?

Ah, retirement dreams! We look forward to that time of life when we won't have to report to work every day, when we can kick back, relax and enjoy "the good life." The good life means something different from person to person and from couple to couple. Things people dream of doing during retirement are as varied as the people themselves. But for many of us, travel is included as part of the retirement plan. We want to be adventurous, travel to places we've always wanted to see, return to places where we vacationed in the past and visit friends and relatives in far off places.

A recreational vehicle helped to fulfill my dream of traveling in retirement. As a matter of fact, to date, I've been to more places in this country than I ever thought possible. I've seen hundreds of sites that, in the past, I'd only read about! All this travel has been achievable and affordable because of the RV.

When my husband first brought up the idea of selling our traditional "stick house" home and moving into a "motor" home, I was flabbergasted. This being our second marriage, our backgrounds were somewhat different. My idea of camping was a resort hotel, while he was more familiar with RVs, trailers, camping and traveling in a recreational vehicle. So we researched options and discussed the "RV retirement" idea thoroughly before arriving at a decision.

Not knowing whether we'd successfully adjust to full-time life in a motor home, we agreed to try it for a year. We sold the house and put the money in the bank, then set out to go RVing for a year. At the end of the 12-month period, if either of us decided the full-time RV lifestyle was not working, we'd buy a house, settle in and use the RV for part-time travel.

Here are a few facts that convinced me to try RVing:

- Because I have wanderlust, extensive travel is very appealing.

- Traveling in an RV eliminates many inconveniences associated with other travel modes. Packing/unpacking and schlepping suitcases in and out of hotels is a thing of the past. Our clothes are with us all the time, neatly hanging in the closet or folded/stacked into drawers; we don't have to worry about forgetting the toothbrush or hair spray.

- Road travelers don't have to deal with the hassles associated with air travel – passenger screening, changing planes and being at the mercy of their schedules.

- The motor home tows a dinghy, so no more rental cars.

- The RV allows us to set our own schedules and itineraries. RVers go when they feel like it and stay wherever they want for as long as they want.

- Wherever we are, we're home. We sleep in our own bed and have our own favorite pillows. We're sure the bathroom is clean. We enjoy home cooked meals on board or outdoors prepared on our barbeque.

- Our cat would be able to travel with us; pets are welcomed at campgrounds.

But the single fact that really convinced me to try the RV lifestyle was this:

- We would be able to see my grown children and grandchildren more often. That did it! At the time we began retirement, seven young grandchildren in three families were living in three different states hundreds of miles apart. Being a typical Granny, I longed to see the little darlings more frequently than I was able. The idea of several shorter visits each year (rather than a two-week stint once a year) was appealing. Being able to spend more time with the children and grandchildren was the major selling point!

Sometime toward the end of the first year on the road we were in Arizona for a couple of months. Out of curiosity, we went to look at a new 55+ community. It was one of those deals where the developer invited prospective buyers to spend the weekend in a guest home, enjoy the amenities, play golf and listen to a sales presentation. Later my husband asked if I wanted to consider buying one of these lovely brand new site-built homes. My response was, "No way! I'm having too much fun. I love my home on wheels!" Quite a transformation from the individual who – just a year ago – didn't know the first thing about RVing.

Although we are partial to full-time RVing, this book recognizes that full-timing is not for everyone. As a matter of fact, most people who utilize an RV in retirement do so on a part-time basis. Owning an RV gives retirees the flexibility to live in the RV for as much or as little time as they want – from extended vacation trips – to half a year or more – to full time.

If you are considering retiring to an RV – either full time or part time – this book is for you. It outlines the major aspects of the RV lifestyle for retirees, and shares ideas and experiences gleaned from many retirees already on the road.

I hope you find the information in this book to be of interest and value as you embark on your exciting Retirement Adventure.

A Word About Endorsements

The purpose of this book is to impart information that will help you make well-informed decisions about RVs and RVing. It is not intended to endorse or recommend any specific products or services. This book doesn't try to sell you anything. But it does give you a broad base of well-researched, current facts about RVs, the RV lifestyle and the products and services RV travelers need and want. *Online Resources* listed throughout are meant to be suggestive only. Final purchase decisions are always yours.

As you go through the text, you'll get a sense that RVers are a friendly and helpful group. They like to talk about places they've been and the best ways to get there. They love to show off their rigs, share information about the latest "new toys," and compare notes on just about any topic, from dumps to dinghys...from itineraries to insurance...from recipes to road conditions and virtually everything else related to RV travel.

RVers never seem to run out of conversation starters. More than most, they enjoy giving advice...and it's generally offered in a spirit of friendship. So, when you're out there, don't hesitate to ask experienced RVers for help and/or information.

When you're mulling over purchases get enough information to make an educated decision. Many good RV forums are up and running on the Internet where you can go and type in a question, ask for advice or start a conversation. You'll get more comments, opinions and facts than you bargained for...and fresh perspectives that will surprise you. Look for the listings of the most popular Clubs and RV Forum Communities in the *Online Resources* at the end of the book.

Chapter 1

Travel: A Retirement Dream

"…You got to have a dream, if you don't have a dream
How you gonna have a dream come true?"
— *Oscar Hammerstein II*

It is not uncommon in this country today for retirees to head out for an adventure on the road. It could be six months, a year or several years…whatever they decide will be the fulfillment of their retirement dream. Currently, about ten percent of people who are over 55 own an RV and the numbers are increasing as more Americans retire. Here are some of the most common ways of utilizing an RV in retirement.

Full-Timers – Adventurous Nomads

Sell the house or vacate the apartment and move into a motor home or fifth-wheel trailer full time. To some this may seem like an extreme lifestyle change. But there are many folks who do it – estimated at about one million. This is an estimate since it is difficult for the census to accurately count the full-timers (it's like aiming at a moving target). Full-timing is the most cost-effective way to use a recreational vehicle in retirement. For comfortable full-time living, one would want to buy a larger, roomier rig. And, while these RVs are among the most expensive, the cost incurred is offset by the savings accrued by not maintaining another home.

Full-time life on the road is wonderfully uncomplicated. Even rising gasoline prices can be factored in because full-timers no longer have to be concerned about property taxes, gas & electric bills, home heating and other property maintenance expenses. The trade-off is advantageous.

Making the transition to full-time RV living is not difficult. It just takes planning. Detailed information is included in Chapter 8. In addition, it is prudent to carefully consider the capability, compatibility and affordability issues outlined in this book before making the decision to go RVing full-time.

Many full-timers are newly retired persons who decide to spend a year or two, or more, as full-time travelers before settling into a retirement domicile. Some use this time to take their "dream trip of a lifetime," the longest vacation they ever had! Others will hit the road for a couple of years to explore different areas of the country in order to decide where they want to settle down for retirement. Others plan to stay on the road until they get tired of traveling or until health or some other issues force them to hang up the keys. If full-time RV living in retirement is suitable for you, your happiest and most rewarding days and years lie ahead.

Then there are those who say, "I could never give up my house. My roots are here," or "I've accumulated so much stuff over the years, what would I do with it all?" or "I need to have a place so the kids and grandkids can come for Sunday dinner and holidays." Others maintain they'd find an RV too confining for all 365 days of the year but they would enjoy shorter trips. For them, part-time RVing may be an option.

How to Become a Snow Bird

A recreational vehicle is perfect for snow birds who want to live in their established home during spring and summer, and move to a warmer climate during the winter months, or vice versa. When snow birds migrate to the alternate seasonal home base, they drive there in the RV, set it up and reside in it for the six months or whatever part of the year they will be there. More often than not, the trips back and forth are planned for a slow relaxing drive, generally not the most direct route, but rather one with inviting and interesting stops along the way.

Popular seasonal destinations for RVing snow birds looking for a place to roost are located in Florida, Texas, Arizona and California. In Florida, snow birds are all over the central and southern parts of the state. In Texas, they head for the Rio Grande Valley. In Arizona, it's The Valley of the Sun – Phoenix, Scottsdale, Mesa area. The population in Arizona swells by more than 400,000 in season each year. Flocks of snow birds are migrating to Mesa, Tucson, Casa Grande and Yuma. In California, migrating snow birds generally land in Imperial, Riverside and San Diego Counties.

In the Southeast, seasonal residents can be found in South Carolina as well as along the Gulf coast in Alabama, Mississippi and Louisiana.

Snow birds congregate in RV parks featuring activities designed specifically for the 55 and older crowd. Golf, tennis, swimming, shuffleboard, bocce ball, billiards, horseshoes and bicycling are among the recreational activities. Many snow bird, age-qualified RV parks can be classified as upscale resorts with amenities such as a pool, spa, restaurant, lounge, hair salon, bingo and live shows. They also feature entertainment, special events, dancing and meeting rooms for clubs of varying interests such as computers, book discussions, arts and crafts, a community orchestra…and more. Snow birds can rent or own their sites at these RV parks.

Some snow birds pack up and head for the warm climates, but move around from park to park and state to state. When we first went on the road, we explored snow bird parks in Arizona one winter, and – in subsequent years – California, Texas and Florida.

Part-Time / Extended-Time Travelers

Other RV retirees take extended trips, either during the summer season or for a few weeks at a time several times a year. They satisfy their desire to travel, yet maintain a permanent home and spend somewhat more time in the home community than the typical snow bird. These are generally people whose family is still nearby and who want to maintain active social, business or community contacts in the home base area.

We've met many couples whose RV travel is somewhat of a compromise. In some cases one wants to hit the road full-time and be the classic nomad, while the other is more attached to the home base and doesn't want to permanently leave. So they plan their time and travels to satisfy both people.

Part time RVing gives retirees the flexibility to utilize the RV for whatever suits their style and needs: for traveling to and living in a seasonal location or for just traveling around the country. Affordability is a key issue to consider, however. Retirees who want to enjoy the RV lifestyle and maintain a land-locked dwelling at the same time need to take a close look at their total combined monthly expenses.

Following the Sun

Life in a recreational vehicle lends itself to warm, mild climates. Therefore, wintertime finds many RVers in the broad swath of Sun Belt states. In summer, RVers travel north to enjoy the great scenic beauty of the lakes and mountains and to escape the oppressive July/August heat of the south.

Online Resources

RV Lifestyle

www.gorving.com
Comprehensive information about the RV lifestyle and activities. Find RV dealers, manufacturers, rentals, campgrounds and more. Free "Go RVing" newsletter is available.

Snow Bird Destinations

www.arizonaguide.com
Official website of the Arizona Office of Tourism.

www.visitcalifornia.com
California's official tourism website.

www.visitflorida.com
Florida's official tourism and travel planning website

www.traveltex.com
The official Texas Tourism website.

Chapter 2

Capability and Compatibility

"One of this country's most precious freedoms is
the freedom to travel…American enthusiasm for
travel is rooted deep in our pioneer heritage."
— *John K. Hanson*
Founder, Winnebago Industries

Most RV retirees have had some experience with or at least exposure to camping. So there is a familiarity with the lifestyle. But there are even more retirees (or near-retirees) who are considering living in an RV for the first time.

These days, with newer, modern and roomy "big rigs" coming on the market, RVing is an attractive retirement option for people who never experienced the RV lifestyle.

Interior of a Condo on Wheels
Courtesy Arina P Habich/Shutterstock.com.

Motor homes and fifth wheel trailers have evolved to vehicles with double, triple and quadruple slideouts. Many of these modern recreational vehicles are aptly called COWs (condos on wheels). It can easily be said: this is not your father's camper.

Current market research data show that RVs are increasingly viewed as status symbols. RVs are in vogue these days after being out of fashion for several decades. Baby boomers are showing a penchant for retiring earlier, traveling more and doing both in style.

From a practical perspective, it is wise to examine your capabilities and preferences to determine whether RVing is a good match for you as a retiree, whether traveling solo or as a couple. Here are a few capability and compatibility issues to consider:

Can I Really Drive It?

If you already have good basic driving skills, it won't be difficult to adjust to driving the large vehicle. Most RVs have power steering, power brakes and automatic transmission. But RV drivers will need to actively improve and sharpen their skills in these areas:

- Learn to adjust and use all mirrors. Set your flat mirrors so you can see the trailer in the first one inch of the mirror, with the rest of the mirror being reserved for your view backwards and to the sides. Get someone to walk around your rig so you can identify the "blind spots."

- Make turns wide enough to accommodate the vehicle's size. When you first start driving the RV, practice in a large empty parking lot. Place cones or boxes and practice making right turns to see if you can come close to the cones without hitting them. Practice maneuvering the vehicle and simulating turns.

- Allow more time to accelerate, slow down and brake. Practice accelerating and braking on a back road or street where there is no risk of accident. This will give you an opportunity to get a feel for the vehicle and learn how much space is needed to safely merge into traffic.

- Always back up very carefully; have someone to guide you whenever possible. Again, practice in a large, empty parking lot. Practice communicating with the individual who will guide you while backing up. (Many couples use walkie-talkie style radios.) Learn the turning radius. Backing up is a skill acquired through practice. You'll need it for getting into campsites. However, backing up in all other situations should be avoided because of the many blind spots around your rig. Take your cue from school bus drivers who are taught to never back up because of the limited visibility around the bus. Also, if you are towing a dinghy four wheels down, you should not back up.

Currently, a commercial driver's license is not required to drive an RV. However, it's a good idea to check licensing requirements with the RV dealer. Some states require a special license for very large RVs while other jurisdictions might add special RV licenses in the future.

Do You Enjoy Driving?

Do you like to drive? Like road trips? Are you comfortable behind the wheel? Do you enjoy mapping out trips via the interstates, highways and byways of America? As a couple do you enjoy traveling together? While it's suggested that both people of a traveling duo know how to drive the RV, typically one enjoys driving more than the other. And, it goes without saying, if you routinely exceed speed limits, you have no business driving in an RV. When you're on the interstates, kick it back to 50-55 mph, relax, and take the stress out of your trip. That's what retirement in an RV is all about!

Attitude is the key to enjoying road trips. Be sure you're both in favor of RVing. Sally, a retired friend, wants desperately to travel by RV to see the country and to visit her grown children in Utah and Ohio. She wants to fuel her wanderlust by getting a trailer to pull with their SUV for a few month-long trips a year. But her husband hates driving and, even as a passenger, tends to get grumpy on road trips. Even though Sally says she is willing to do all the driving, she recognizes it just wouldn't work for them.

Simple Mechanical Tasks

A few years ago I was telling a member of our extended family about our RV retirement travels. He remarked how fortunate I was to have a spouse who is "mechanically inclined."

He went on to explain that he's not the handy-man type and has no interest in learning. He always hired people to do the work around the house (even for hanging pictures on the walls). He knows nothing about the technical side of a vehicle and has no interest in learning. And, as he put it, "I'm just not interested in tinkering around a vehicle."

One of the requirements for successful RVing is an interest in and willingness to perform the day-to-day tasks involved. These include hooking up to and disconnecting from the electric, water and sewer outlets at RV Parks…also, properly dumping the grey water and black water (sewer) tanks every few days and filling the fresh water tank. You can't hire someone to do these things for you. One or both of you have to be willing and able to handle these tasks or you won't be able to go RVing. Minor mechanical procedures involved with RVing are not difficult…anyone can do them. And these activities are not necessarily "a guy thing." Many women who go RVing solo handle all the outside household jobs.

First-time RVers can expect detailed instructions from the seller/dealer at the time they purchase an RV. Once you're on the road, you'll find that other RVers are very accommodating. There is a unique camaraderie among RVers all over the country. Don't hesitate to ask for help and advice. You'll learn more from your neighbors in campgrounds than you will from the instruction manuals that came with your rig.

Compatibility

Some years ago, a country song entitled "18 Wheels & A Dozen Roses" told the story of a trucker who had just retired after 30 years of driving the interstates. The song speaks to how much the trucker is looking forward to spending the rest of his life with the one he loves. Hence, the dozen roses. The lyrics sing, "…They'll buy a Winnebago, set out to find America…they'll do a lot of catchin' up, a little at a time. With pieces of the old dream, they're gonna light the old flame." Sounds romantic, doesn't it? Let's hope the trucker and his wife are compatible enough to have that idyllic environment in their Winnebago retirement home.

Every couple has their own unique relationship. Consider whether yours is suited to traveling and living in a small home on wheels. Do you travel well together? Do you share the wanderlust and sense of adventure? In our travels we've met literally hundreds of couples on the road and they all seem to have certain qualities in common. Usually they are best friends who genuinely like each other and have shared values. They are easy-going, don't take themselves too seriously and rarely argue. This doesn't mean that RVing couples don't disagree, but it is very unusual to hear them raising voices to one another. Successful RVing couples seem to have developed the ability to disagree without being disagreeable. They are direct, polite, honest, caring and forgiving.

Although they spend virtually 24/7 together, successful RVing couples figure out how to give each other space. One man says he enjoys the first couple of hours each day. He is an "early bird" who usually can't sleep beyond 5:30 or 6:00. So he makes the coffee, does his morning meditation and prayer, reads the paper, watches his favorite morning TV show and occasionally will go out for a walk. By the time his wife the "night owl" awakes at 8:00 his day is off to a great start – he's had his private time. His wife likes the routine because she gets to sleep in. She says if she has to arise at the crack of dawn she will be cranky. When she is ready for some space, she will head for the public library (every town has one) for a few hours, or she'll go out to the nearest shopping mall. Other RVers will get their private time by sometimes doing routine activities solo such as laundry, shopping, biking or walking.

We know a couple who have been married for more than 50 years. Paul and Kate are still on the road; they started full-time RVing 15 years ago. They genuinely like each other and still hold hands when they're walking from their motor home to the recreation hall. They are a cheerful couple who enjoy life and the people around them. They always make the time to ask friends (old and new) to "come on over and sit a spell." They are an inspiration! On the other hand, we once met a couple who had been full-timing for a few years when the husband – out of the blue – insisted it was time to put the rig up for sale and go back to Ohio because he "absolutely needed" to have his house and yard. His wife was in tears; she didn't want to give up RVing. But for her husband, at that point, there would be no discussion. It appeared he went along with full-time RVing to please his wife and, after some time, simmering dissatisfaction with the lifestyle rose to the surface. Don't do that to yourselves. If you decide to go RVing – full time or extended time – make it a point to re-visit that decision from time to time to be sure you're both on the same page with the lifestyle choice.

The habit patterns of a relationship – be they positive or negative – don't happen overnight. Couples whose relationships are suited to RVing find the lifestyle has enriched their relationship immeasurably. But don't be fooled into thinking RVing will repair a faltering relationship. Side by side traveling in an enclosed space could exacerbate it.

Survey Says...

Many tens of thousands of long-time RVing couples continue to have enjoyable and fulfilling experiences on the road. Why did they decide to take up RVing? Why do they continue to enjoy it many years later? An informal survey produced these answers from veteran RV retirees:

- My spouse and I are best friends; we get along very well and have fun together.

- We enjoy traveling and we can afford to do it.

- RVing is the most relaxing and the least stressful way for older people to travel. We don't like to be at the mercy of airline schedules.

- Now that we're retired, we don't need to go anywhere in a hurry. When we have to be at an event in another state, we plan ahead and give ourselves plenty of time to get there.

- Our preference is to see our own country. Neither of us has a desire to go abroad.

- Our hobbies are consistent with the traveling lifestyle.

- There's an incredible sense of freedom in RVing.

- We love meeting new people.

- Road trips are (and have always been) our favorite way to travel.

- We're grateful for what we have; all our needs are met and life is good.

- We like to travel but don't want to leave the dog behind; our pet travels with us!

Online Resources

RV Driving School

www.rvschool.com

Learn how to drive or tow your RV from certified instructors. Training available at several locations across the U.S. Seminars offered all year.

RV Lifestyle

www.doityourselfrv.com

RV enthusiasts share the best the Internet has to offer about how to make the most of your RV. Good information and click on the "Funny" tab for a good laugh.

Did you know...

There are more than four million miles of roads and over 16,000 campgrounds in the United States. Adventurous RVers have a lot of exploring to do.

Chapter 3

Affordability

> "It is good to have money and the things money can buy,
> but it's good too, to check up once in a while and
> make sure you haven't lost the things money can't buy."
> — *George Lorimer*

Can I Afford It?

Can I/we afford to go RVing in retirement? Are we ready financially? This chapter is not intended to provide professional financial advice. I am not an accountant and we are not rich. Neither of us is a financial expert. But we do know our own circumstance…and we're frugal. When we first considered this question, we kept it simple: "Will we have enough money coming in to cover the money going out?"

To answer affordability questions, take an inventory; get out a pencil, paper and calculator or make a simple (or a complex one if that's your style) spread sheet. List retirement fixed income on one side and estimated expenses on the other. Prepare a separate list of assets in your "nest egg" section.

Here are a few tips to consider as you review the numbers:

- Be aware that an RV will depreciate in value almost from the moment you drive it off the dealer's property. It is not prudent to spend the entire proceeds from the sale of real estate on a new vehicle.

- Remember that, as retirees, you will have a fixed income – no annual raise or generous year-end bonus in future years.

- The earlier you plan to retire, the larger your nest egg needs to be.

- Be generous when estimating expenses. I overestimate, especially on medical costs, so as to have a cushion. Don't rush and be thorough in listing all your anticipated expenses.

- In retirement, long-range planning is not nearly as "long" range as it was when we were young. But we do need to think about and plan for our life expectancy. Money should be allocated for current and future large purchases…a house, a car, etc.

- If you plan to be a full-timer for just a year or two or for the rest of your life, consider that unexpected situations (such as illness) might force you to settle down in one place.

- If you plan to be a snow bird or a part-time RVer on your own schedule, be sure to account for expenses to carry your home base as well as the RV. Even though you have a fully paid-for home, you still have expenses such as property tax, utilities and maintenance costs. These don't go away while you're away. Also figure in the cost of storing the RV while you're in your land-locked house.

Income / Expense Chart

The chart below is a suggested outline for a budget that will allow you to determine whether RVing is affordable. For those planning to go RVing full-time, some expense categories may not apply. But, the chart will also accommodate those budgets that must cover the expenses of both a stick-built permanent home and an RV. Use the categories that apply to your situation, then add 'em up.

Next list assets in your "nest egg." This list should include assets you do not plan to draw on immediately as a source of retirement income.

Monthly Income

This list includes estimates of income that will be received on a regular basis and used to cover day-to-day expenses when you retire. If you haven't started collecting Social Security, reference your most recent annual statement estimates. List pensions and any other periodic payments you expect to receive in retirement.

Social Security   _____

Social Security   _____

Pension   _____

Pension   _____

Pension   _____

Disability Payment   _____

Annuity Payment   _____

Income from Trust   _____

Interest/Dividends   _____

Rental property income   _____

Other   _____

Total Monthly Income: _____

Monthly Expenses

Clothing/Sundries – Includes clothes, shoes, personal items, cosmetics, hair cuts, etc. **Entertainment** – Think about cruises, theater, movies, golf, casino gaming, tennis, fitness club, etc. **Food** – Grocery/supermarket and dining out expenses. **Gifts/Donations** – Christmas, birthdays, church donations.

Clothing/Sundries   _____

Entertainment   _____

Food   _____

Gifts/Donations   _____

Housing:

This category includes mortgage payment on the stick-built house (if applicable) and an RV loan (if any). Also include campground fees; use an approximate rate of $30 per night if you'll be in a campground every night, you may be able to knock the average down to $25 a night if you will do the free overnight parking thing a few times a month. (More on this topic in Chapter 7.) Snow birds should figure on $800 to $1,000 per month for rent during the winter season. Also include in this category campground memberships (if applicable), club dues, rally fees and mailbox rental (if full-time or extended-time).

Mortgage   _____

RV Loan   _____

Camping Fees   _____

Club dues/rallies   _____

Other   _____

Insurance:

Vehicles   _____

Home   _____

Other   _____

Medical Expenses:

A major expense in retirement. Medical insurance might be more expensive if you retire prior to becoming Medicare eligible. And, even after age 65, Medicare and supplementary premium costs are rising, and there are out-of-pocket expenses. You may want to "pad" this line to account for escalating costs.

Insurance Premiums   _____

Drugs   _____

Other   _____

Taxes:

Federal   _____

State   _____

Real Estate   _____

Other   _____

Travel:

Calculate how many miles you plan to travel in the RV and figure gas prices on the high side so they won't blow your budget if they rise sharply in the future. Maintenance includes routine maintenance on the vehicles plus tires, brakes, etc. Annual fees include vehicle registrations and drivers license renewals.

Gas   _____

Maintenance   _____

Fees   _____

Utilities:

Include estimated utility costs for land-locked residence(s) as well as the RV. This includes gas, electric, water, phone, cable, lawn care, cleaning services and association fees (if applicable).

Phone (including wireless)   _____

Internet Service   _____

Gas & Electric   _____

TV (cable/dish)   _____

Lawn Maintenance   _____

Other   _____

Other	_____

Total Monthly Expenses:	_____

Assets in the Nest Egg

Real Estate	_____

Other property	_____

Tax Deferred Account	_____

Tax Deferred Account	_____

Other investments	_____

Total Assets in the Nest Egg:	_____

Nest Egg Calculation

List assets you own that you don't plan to draw on as a source of regular income when you initially retire. List the potential selling price of your home less the balance of any mortgage(s). Include tax-deferred accounts such as 401k, 503b and IRAs as well as other savings and investments.

Here's where you'll want to do some planning. On the income/expense chart you determined your initial monthly budget. Now consider your mortality. Thanks to dramatic increases in life expectancy, nowadays people can plan for 20 or more years of retirement. Although the cost of living has been fairly stable in recent years, there's always the possibility that prices will rise in the future. Medical expenses are apt to increase as we age.

How will you fund the big items – RV, car, home? When you begin shopping for an RV, you'll find there's a rig to fit every budget. Be prudent. You want to enjoy life during retirement, but you'll also want to ensure you won't outlive your resources. If you think you'll need to buy one of the big items – such as a car or stick-built home – in the future, set the money aside for it now, if possible.

Be judicious in spending large one-time distributions. Our friend Tommy decided to accept an early retirement offer from his company some years ago. At age 55, he had a couple of options – either a fixed moderate monthly payment for the rest of his life or a single sum "buy-out." The buy-out amount was more money than Tommy had ever seen at one time. He took it, bought a luxury motor coach and put the rest of the money into an account managed by a consultant who assured Tommy there was enough money to provide a steady retirement income. This was in the middle of the high-flying 90s. The payments flowed into his checking account as promised and Tommy and his wife enjoyed a few years of excellent travel in their fancy motor home. Then came a dip in the stock market and Tommy's big account suddenly became a very small account. Now the nest egg was too small to continue providing the income they relied on. Fortunately, the motor home was fully paid-for and Tommy and the Mrs. were in good health. So they stayed on the road and took advantage of the many job opportunities available in campgrounds and RV resorts. They are still enjoying the RV lifestyle.

You don't necessarily need a very large income to go RVing. People at all income levels can savor the RV lifestyle. And, people who want to continue working will find there are many job opportunities on the road. Chapter 12 covers the "working on the road" topic in greater detail.

Did you know...

The term RV (recreational vehicle) wasn't coined until the 1960's. Until then, all units were either campers or trailers.

Chapter 4

What Kind of Rig

"…I take to the open road,
Healthy, free, the world before me,
The long brown path before me,
leading wherever I choose."
— *Walt Whitman*

The term RV—recreational vehicle—covers a broad spectrum of homes-on-wheels that provide the convenience of travel and living quarters all in the same vehicle. Before I became an RVer, I would see these vehicles on the road and wonder: Who are these nomads? Where are they going? Is it hard to drive that behemoth? What does it look like on the inside? What's it like to be living in there?

RVs can range in size from a small place for sleeping and eating to large luxurious units featuring multiple slideouts with full bedroom, bathroom, kitchen, dining area and living room. All come completely furnished.

This section provides an overview and pictures of the basic RV types. RVs fall into two general categories – towable and motorized.

Towables

Most early recreational vehicles were trailers. They were developed in the 20th century after cars became common; trailers were a low-cost way to take a road trip vacation. The first generation of trailers didn't have sewage systems, consequently campgrounds provided shower and bathroom facilities…as many campgrounds still do today.

In listing towables, we begin with the two smallest, most inexpensive units, generally used by first-time campers or families with young children. The Folding Camper Trailer

(Pop-Up) and the Truck Camper are described here for active retirees interested in roughing it.

Folding Camper Trailer: This is a lightweight unit towable by an SUV or, in some cases, by the family car. On the road it is an 8 to 15-foot shallow box; upon arrival at a campsite, it opens up and out to a unit with canvas sides resembling a tent on a flatbed with sleeping, dining, kitchen and bathroom. The unit is easy to store in a garage. Prices for pop-ups range from $5,000 to $22,000.

Folding Camper Trailer (Pop-Up Trailer)

Truck Camper: Technically not a towable, this unit loads onto the bed or chassis of many pickups. It is good for traveling to remote camping areas. Some truck camper units do not have toilets and showers, although the more expensive units are fully self-contained. Prices range from $4,000 to $26,000. Be sure to check the pickup's gross vehicle weight restraints before attaching a truck camper.

Conventional Travel Trailers: Travel trailers can be towed by SUVs, vans and pickups. Conventional trailers are listed here separately from fifth wheels. Fifth wheels (often called 5ers) are also trailers, but they have a unique configuration, characterized by the way they are attached to the tow vehicle.

Conventional travel trailers range in size from 12 to 35 feet. They are attached to the tow vehicle with a bumper or frame hitch. All but the smallest trailers need to be pulled with

Truck Camper

a special load distributing hitch and a sway bar under it. There are many lightweight trailers on the market.

Trailer interiors range in style from simple to more luxurious. Many include slideouts in either the living room or bedroom area or both. After the trailer is set on a campsite and hooked up, the tow vehicle is unhitched and can be used for local transportation. Travel trailers range in price from $8,000 to $95,000. Although travel trailers are generally

Travel Trailer

cost-efficient, they have a few disadvantages. Longer travel trailers may be difficult to handle on interstates when it's windy or when being passed by large trucks. Most travel trailers do not have generators, although a stand-alone generator can be added (could be noisy). Also, the trailer cannot be accessed while the vehicle is traveling. It is illegal for anyone to travel inside the trailer while it is in motion.

Fifth Wheel Travel Trailer: This special type of trailer is built to be towed by a pickup with a unique hitch mounted on the bed of the pickup. A fifth wheel (5er) has an extension on the front of the trailer box that extends over the bed of the tow vehicle and a horizontal plate that looks like a wheel that rests on the tow vehicle for support. This plate is where the fifth wheel gets its name. The hitch places the load in the center of the tow vehicle axles instead of behind it and gives the rig better maneuverability.

Fifth Wheel Trailer

Most fifth wheel trailers are spacious and have multiple push button slide-outs that can expand the interior space from 8 feet to as much as 14 feet. All fifth wheel trailers are bi-level units with lots of space, fully self-contained and furnished. Usually the sleeping area and bathroom are over the truck bed, allowing for more living space on the main level. The center portion of the fifth wheel generally contains a kitchen with the latest in appliances, dining and living room areas. Fifth wheels range in length from 21 to 40 feet and they are usually roomier than conventional trailers. Their price range is from $18,000 to $160,000 and higher.

A fifth wheel trailer is easier to handle than a conventional travel trailer. However, it requires a heavy duty truck to pull it. As with other towables, the living unit cannot be accessed while the trailer is traveling. A fifth wheel always has the split-level floor plan, so people who wish to have an RV with the interior all on a single level should opt for a conventional travel trailer.

Sport Utility Trailer: This is a specialized trailer designed to have living quarters plus a built-in garage for storing cycles, ATVs and other sports vehicles or equipment. It can be either a conventional trailer or a fifth wheel. The garage at the back of the unit has a fold-down door specifically designed to house all the owner's "toys." The front of the trailer has sleeping, dining and bathroom facilities. The trailer also has electric and water systems. These units can be 16 to 40 feet in length and range in price from $10,300 to $170,000.

Sport Utility Trailer

Motorized

Class A: This classic motor home most resembles a bus. It is entirely built on a truck chassis that was especially designed for motor homes. It provides a smooth, stable ride and is powered by either a gas-fueled engine or a diesel-fueled engine. It is easy to drive. Most motor homes have push-button slideout sections that expand the living space. Some have multiple slideouts. The inside of a Class A is spacious and has a living room, kitchen, dinette, bedroom and bathroom. Motor home coaches have all the creature comforts – modern furnishings, up-to-date appliances, and some have washer/dryer units and dishwashers.

Because of the size of most motor homes – and the time-consuming process of hooking up at campgrounds – it is not practical to travel in a Class A unit without a towed vehicle. Most motor home owners tow a dinghy (or "toad" as it's often called) to use for transportation after the motor home is set up at an RV park or campground. Class A motor homes range in price from about $70,000 to $900,000 and more. On average, gas models cost between $100,000 and $200,000 and diesels are higher in price, generally from $200,000 and up. Class A motor homes range in size from 24 to 45 feet long. Big rigs are the most favored RV of full-timers. A key advantage is accessibility to the interior of the unit while traveling. Motor homes permit passenger movement throughout the RV while riding; towable trailers require stopping in order to enter the living area.

Class A Motor Home

Class B – Van Camper: This vehicle looks like a regular van with an elevated roofline, but packs a lot into a small space. Typically, it is between 16 and 21 feet in length making it versatile, maneuverable and economical. The Class B vehicle drives like a heavily loaded van…which is exactly what it is. The van camper usually provides sleeping, kitchen and

Class B Van Camper

bathroom facilities. It forces people to travel light, as there's very little storage room on board. Most van campers have electric and water hookups. The Class B vehicle usually does not tow a dinghy. It can double as the vehicle used to get around town once you pull into a campground or an RV park for a few days or longer. However, you need to break camp every time you go out. The price range is $60,000 to $130,000.

Class C – Mini Motor Home: This motor home is built on a van frame. Its most recognizable feature is the attached section over the cab that can be used for extra sleeping room or for storage. Like the Class A, the Class C is a fully self-contained unit. It has living room, kitchen and dining area plus bedroom and bathroom facilities. Most Class C units come with push-button slideouts that enlarge the living quarters. But they have less storage and weight capacity than do Class A's. Class C units are capable of towing a dinghy, and many do. Prices range approximately from $45,000 to $200,000 and sizes can range from 20 to 36 feet in length.

Class C Mini Motor Home

Industry Standards

Whatever vehicle(s) you decide to buy, check to be sure the manufacturer is an RVIA (Recreation Vehicle Industry Association) member. This will ensure that the manufacturer meets all current codes and standards. RVIA manufacturers self-certify compliance with over 500 safety specifications for electrical, plumbing, heating and fire and life safety established under the American National Standards Institute (ANSI) A119.2 Standard of Recreation Vehicles. As a condition of RVIA membership, manufacturers are subject to periodic unannounced plant inspections by RVIA representatives to audit their compliance with ANSI standards.

Online Resources

Manufacturers

www.rvia.org
Directory of Recreation Vehicle Industry Association member manufacturers.

www.rversonline.org
The *Info Resources* section has links to major RV manufacturers.

RV Shows

www.rvia.org
Recreation Vehicle Industry Association (RVIA) website. Has the current calendar of RV shows throughout the U.S. and Canada. Also has information about the various styles of RVs.

www.thebestrvshow.com
California RV Show, called "the Granddaddy of shows." Held every October.

www.chicagorvshow.com
Largest show in the Midwest.

Did you know...

The RV industry ranks as one of the most American of industries. More than 75% of all recreational vehicles are produced in the U.S. by American companies employing American workers.

Chapter 5

What Kind of Tow Vehicle or Toad?

"I go where I'm towed."
"Be patient. I'm pushing this big motor home."
— *Signs seen on toads.*

Definitions: Tow Vehicle and Toad

No matter what kind of rig you drive, it will likely involve two separate vehicles.

> Tow vehicle. If your RV is a towable trailer, you'll need a vehicle with which to tow it. That's the "tow vehicle."

> Toad. If your RV is motorized, likely you will be towing another vehicle behind it. That's called a "toad" (or sometimes referred to as a dinghy).

Tow Vehicles and Their Hitches

There's a lot of information out there about tow vehicles. It is vitally important that you do your own research and gather information from many sources. The primary source is, of course, the vehicle manufacturer's specifications. Also, speak with experienced RVers. If you don't know any, log on to one of the RV forums on the Internet and post a question. Filter through all the information and draw your own conclusions. This gives you the best shot at making an educated decision about the tow vehicle best suited for your situation. We've heard far too many stories about people who relied on assurances from a sales person that a particular tow vehicle would easily be able to handle a trailer only to find out it could not.

Be a well-informed consumer. Have a good basic understanding of the weight ratings of tow vehicles. In general, they can be categorized as:

Light duty vehicles – such as SUVs, mini-vans and light duty trucks, usually have ratings up to 3,500 pounds.

Medium duty vehicles – half-ton trucks fall into this category that has approximate ratings to 5,000 pounds.

Heavy duty vehicles – three-quarter and one ton trucks with ratings up to 10,000 pounds.

Super heavy duty vehicles – those designed specifically to handle the heavier weights.

There are other features that some drivers look for in a tow vehicle such as dual axles, tandem wheels, pulling power and short or long bed on the truck. Tow vehicles can be powered by either gasoline or diesel.

Matching the tow vehicle to the trailer is critical to the overall safety of the rig. The two important issues to consider are weight and connection. If your truck is underrated for your trailer, get either a bigger truck or a smaller trailer. Make sure your hitch is rated to tow your trailer or fifth wheel.

Tow vehicles will have manufacturer's specifications of:

1) Tow capacity – acceptable weight range of the vehicle to be towed and,

2) GCVW – gross combined vehicle weight of both the tow vehicle and the trailer, including cargo and people.

So, first you need to know what your truck weighs loaded. Second, subtract the truck weight from the GCVW in the manufacturer's specs to get your desired trailer weight. When calculating the trailer weight your truck can pull, start with the UVW (unloaded vehicle weight) and add cargo load (clothing, household items, etc.). Include weights of full tanks (water tanks weigh in at 8.3 pounds per gallon). After that, use the 80% rule of thumb. That is, tow only up to 80% of the maximum. That's the way professional over the road truckers do it. This allows for wind, traffic, steep grades and emergencies.

Pay close attention to weight. As a friend who pulls a trailer told me, "Don't send a boy to do a man's job." If the tow vehicle is too light, crosswinds on the interstate can be mighty scary. Towing a heavy trailer with a lightweight vehicle makes the tail wag the dog.

There are many types of trailer hitches available and just about as many opinions about what's the best one to use. Always calculate the weight of a fully-loaded conventional trailer or fifth wheel trailer before buying the hitch and be sure the hitch is rated for your trailer's fully loaded weight.

The conventional trailer hitch should be straight and level. Leveling bars and a sway control bar are helpful. For fifth wheel trailers the pin receiver is mounted in the bed of the tow truck and the pin box on the trailer's gooseneck fits into it.

Motorized RVs and Their Toads

Most motor homes you see on the road these days are towing an auxiliary vehicle – commonly referred to as a dinghy or "the toad." It adds convenience to traveling in a motorized vehicle because the toad can be unhitched and used for local transportation after the motor home is hooked up at an RV park or campground.

There are three ways to tow the toad:

- 4-wheels-down,
- on a dolly, or
- in or on a trailer.

Most RVers prefer to tow 4-wheels-down. It is easier to connect/disconnect the 4-down toad. A disadvantage of using a dolly or a trailer is that it is harder to get the car on and off the dolly or trailer. And then there's the problem of where to put the trailer or dolly once the car is off. Many campground sites do not have enough room on a single site for an extra piece of equipment.

Any vehicle with a manual transmission can be towed four-wheels down. However, most people have automatic transmission vehicles. Only a few automatics can be easily towed 4-down. There are other vehicles that can be flat (4-down) towed if certain recommended modifications are made, such as driveshaft disconnects, transmission lube pumps and tow kits installed by authorized dealers. It is very important to check manufacturers' specifications to determine the vehicle's towability. Do not rely on information provided by anyone other than the manufacturer. You could risk doing permanent damage to a vehicle if you attempt to tow a car 4-down that's not towable.

There are three basic factors to consider:

1) Can the vehicle be safely towed flat (according to manufacturer's specs?)

2) What is your motor home's towing weight capacity?

3) Will the combined weight of both vehicles (fully loaded) be within the motor home manufacturer's GCVW rating?

Most Class A's will be OK when you check out and add up the weights. When calculating gross combined vehicle weights, don't forget tanks at 8.3 lbs. per gallon and the people on board at whatever their weights. If you plan to carry heavy stuff in the toad, don't forget to add it to the toad's total weight. If towing with a Class C, do the calculations carefully. Upgrading the hitch will not change the GCVW assigned to the chassis.

There are many effective and easy-to-use hitches available. We do not endorse any particular one. However, we urge you to use a major manufacturer who complies with safety standards and government codes and regulations. Every hitch must have safety chains or cables connected securely to the toad and then crossed under the tow bar before being attached to the hitch receiver.

Braking System Necessary

All trailers should have a braking system that is controlled by a connection to the tow vehicle's braking system. Not so with the toads. Whatever kind of vehicle you decide to tow along behind your motor home will not come equipped with a braking system. Please do not attempt to trailer a car (or any other auxiliary vehicle) behind a motor home without first putting a braking system on it!

The sign on the toad may jokingly read, "Be patient with me. I'm pushing this big motor home!" But let's hope the toad is not actually pushing the larger vehicle. That could be dangerous. Picture this: a big 'ol motor home cruising down the highway at 50 mph on dry pavement has to make a sudden stop. How long does it take to stop?

- 132 feet for a motor home without a toad.

- 137 feet for a motor home with a toad that has a braking system.

- 209 feet for a motor home with a toad that DOES NOT have a braking system.

It is obvious that all vehicles in tow should have a braking system! The braking system (incorporating a break away switch) is essential safety equipment.

Connecting is a Critical Procedure

Connecting and disconnecting a vehicle in tow correctly is critical. Serious accidents have resulted from a poorly connected trailer or dinghy. Learn how to hitch and unhitch properly and be meticulous about following correct procedures. Have a checklist handy the first few times you hitch and unhitch and follow it step-by-step. You'll eventually memorize it. Don't rush…check and double check to be sure all connections are tight. A break-away trailer or dinghy could cause a deadly serious accident, especially on an interstate.

Monitor Weight For Safety Sake

It is very important to know the manufacturer's Gross Combined Vehicle Weight rate and to weigh your vehicle periodically to be sure you do not exceed the GCVW.

Many RVs are overweight. This excess weight causes premature equipment failure or vehicle breakdowns. Even worse, an overweight vehicle can make the driver lose control of the vehicle and cause serious accidents. Many people think that manufacturers design some overcapacity into RVs, but they don't! If an accident happens and the overweight vehicle is shown to be the cause, police officers will issue tickets and the insurance company will not pay claims. Do not take the risk.

Make a note of your GCVW, weigh in periodically and keep the records. Use a CAT (Certified Automated Truck Scale) located at major truck stops. It will give the overall weight of the rig and the weight on each axle. If you do an annual weigh-in, you will be able to note changes in your rig from year to year, i.e., more stuff on board and/or shifting loads. In the first four years on the road we added 1,000 pounds, and only a small percentage of that was the weight gain on the pilot and co-pilot.

Annual Towing Guides

A Guide To Towing is published annually as a supplement to *Trailer Life* magazine. It contains the official trailer-tow ratings for the current year plus helpful information about selecting a tow vehicle, hitching up and much more.

The *Dinghy Towing Guide* is published each year by *MotorHome* magazine. It lists vehicles that have been approved by their manufacturers for towing over long distances without speed restrictions. However, you should always check the owner's manual of the model you are considering. This is the only way to be sure the vehicle can be towed without drive train modifications.

Online Resources

Safety

www.rvsafety.org
Official site of the Recreation Vehicle Safety Education Foundation.

www.catscale.com
Find the location of CAT scales across the U.S.

www.changingears.com
"Departure Checklist for Trailers" available in RV Checklists section.

Towing Guides

www.trailerlife.com
Publishes the annual Trailer Guide; may be printed from the website.

www.motorhomemagazine.com
Publishes the annual Dinghy Towing Guide; available in pdf format ($)

Chapter 6

The Selection Process

"The great thing about fact-based decisions
is that they override the hierarchy."
— *Jeff Bezos*
Internet Entrepeneur

RV Buyer's Most Frequently Asked Question

What's the most frequently-asked question from people who are planning to take their retirement to the road?

Question:

"I just retired and have been trying to decide if I should get a MH (motor home) or go to a 5er (fifth wheel trailer).

We posed the question to some of our friends who are already RVing. Here are a few comments from the experienced RV retirees.

Answers/Comments:

- A 5er is a good choice if I'm gonna stay put for months at a time. But for moving around every week or so, the MH is better.

- We price-compared a brand new pickup, capable of pulling a new 33-foot 5er, to a comparable MH. Both the truck and the 5er cost about $70,000 (no financing). MHs were in the $100,000+ range.

- On the road, the MH is a smoother and more comfortable ride compared to the cab of a pickup truck.

- A shorter MH with a couple of slideouts gives us good living space when we're parked, maneuverability on the road and we can still get into federal and state campgrounds. We tow a dinghy.

- We prefer the 5er. If our truck has a problem, the house doesn't go into the shop. Also, if the truck or the 5er don't work out for us, we only have to replace half of the rig.

- If you move often, stay in a MH. It's easier to set up and take down. Leveling and setting up a trailer takes longer.

- The Mrs. likes the MH. She can get up to use the potty without having to wait till we find a rest area on the interstate or a wide enough space along the road to safely pull over.

- We traded back to a 5er. The MH was a lot of work and expensive to maintain. There's very little maintenance on the 5er and more room inside the home.

- A 5er is cheaper than a MH and it trails better than a TT (travel trailer).

- Day travel is a drawback of a 5er. You're cramped in the cab of a pickup with a 5er. Access to the extra room in a MH is great while we're rolling down the highway.

- A 5er seems more like a house to me. It was a good choice for us snow birds because we stay in one location for six months.

Shop, Shop, Shop

An RV is a major purchase. Entry level units can run from $40,000 to $90,000. But mid-level and high-end motor homes and fifth wheels can be priced into the hundreds of thousands. Now that you've become familiar with the categories of recreational vehicles, it's time to begin shopping. Probably the best advice we can give you for the shopping phase is, "Don't buy too fast!" You certainly don't want to commit to such a large purchase until you're satisfied that you've explored all the options and compared prices. We actually shopped for 10 months before we bought our Class A motor home. Here's how we approached it:

1) Determine the price range we could afford. Not knowing whether I would love RVing or hate it, my husband suggested we stay in the low end of the price ranges. We had decided to buy a new rig (my preference), and we didn't want to take a big hit on the depreciation factor if I didn't like it. So, we set our price range in the neighborhood of the low to mid $100's.

2) Determine what kind of rig to buy. Since we planned to be full-timers for at least a year, we ruled out the smaller camper units and even conventional travel trailers. Thus, our selection process was narrowed down to either a Class A motor coach towing a dinghy or a larger fifth wheel towed with a diesel pickup. Both options gave us a vehicle to drive locally once we were set up at an RV park or campground. Our first shopping foray was to an RV show in Florida where we got to inspect dozens and dozens of rigs, inside and out with no stress, no pressure…just browsing and dreaming. It was fun! We looked at motor homes and 5th wheels, and finally decided on a Class A motor home based on a couple of factors: my husband has a chronic back condition which could not tolerate riding in a truck and I like the idea of having access to the motor home while on the road.

3) What make/what model? At this point the buying process becomes more focused. You can walk into a dealer showroom or go to an RV show and zero in on the type of rig that suits you. Don't rush. Take your purchase seriously.

   If you are looking at towables, consider the trailer or fifth wheel and the tow vehicle as a single unit. Check out the gross vehicle weight and towing capacity of your truck. Sit in the cab and picture yourself driving down the road. Be sure the hitch arrangement for a fifth wheel is compatible with your tow truck. Inspect all areas of the trailer, picture yourself living there. Check out all the rooms and storage spaces.

   If you are looking at motorized rigs, check out every type before narrowing it down to Class A, B or C. Know the carrying capacity in terms of space and weight. Check out the towing capacity for a dinghy. Picture yourself driving in it. If the motor home is displayed with slides out, ask to have the slides in and try out the driver's chair. Can it be adjusted back far enough to suit your needs? Picture yourself living in the unit. Check out the closets and drawers, look at storage bins underneath the rig. Look at the bedroom with the slide(s) in. Is the space practical for staying in tight areas where you won't be able to put your slides out at night? Sit on the commode…you'd be surprised at how important that is, and step into the shower.

Visit many dealers. Test drive the vehicles. Be persistent, ask questions. Take brochures to browse through later. If possible, try to attend RV shows. This will give you an opportunity to see many makes and models of towables and motorized units all in the same place. You can find current dates and locations of RV shows on the RVIA website. When an RV show is planned for your area, you'll usually see local advertising for a month or so before the show.

4) Buy it; don't let yourself be "sold." What in the world does that mean? During the buying process you will meet many sales people who are very anxious to sell you their unit. Please don't fall for, "This great price is for today only; I can't guarantee it tomorrow." When you are close to making a decision, use the "sleep on it" rule. Say, "I want to mull this over tonight and will get back to you tomorrow." The decision to buy the RV is yours and yours alone. Inspect and test drive extensively. After you've done a lot of research and comparative pricing, you will be in a better position to buy the rig that's most suitable for you.

5) New or Used? Obviously, buying a brand new rig is more expensive than buying a used one. But the step-by-step process described here applies to shopping for either a new or a used unit. If you opt for a used vehicle, consider manufacturer's warranties and extended warranties. Depending on the age and mileage, they could be available with the unit. When shopping for a used RV, examine everything very carefully. Be wary of rigs that are older than about 6 or 7 years. They won't have the latest improvements in braking, cooling and suspension systems. They won't feature the most modern

appliances and the latest safety improvements. RV manufacturers are continuously improving all aspects of their rigs.

When you find a used RV that interests you, look up its value in the NADA Guide; this will give you a good idea of whether the asking price is in the ball park. You may also want to consider a professional inspection. When purchasing real estate, the buyer generally hires a "home inspection service" to uncover any major flaws in the property. Why not do the same for real estate on wheels? It is prudent to hire a competent and experienced RV technician to inspect and evaluate the rig prior to purchase.

6) Have fun shopping. I was born to shop, so this is my favorite part. We thoroughly enjoyed the flashy brochures, pouring over floorplans, poking around different rigs, test driving them, going to the RV shows, surfing the net and visiting the websites of various manufacturers. In the end our careful research and comparative shopping paid off. We narrowed our choice down to a specific manufacturer, make, model, floor plan, and interior décor.

One day we walked on to a dealer's lot, and there it was – exactly what we wanted! We test drove it, came back to the lot and told the salesperson, "We'll buy it, if we can agree on a fair price." She was so stunned, it took a few minutes for her to recuperate. We had already done 10 months of research and were ready to negotiate on the price. So the sales person didn't have to "sell" us the motor home…and it's one of the best purchases we ever made!

Trying It Out Before Buying

Once you've determined the type of rig you want to purchase, you might want to rent or borrow one and try it out. Class C and Class A motor homes are the most commonly rented. But, travel trailers are available also. Going out on the road for a few weeks will give you a chance to experience the RV lifestyle and find out what kind of rig best suits your needs. It is a good way to take an extended "test drive."

A few national companies offer modern recreational vehicles for rent. Look them up on the Internet simply by typing in the key words "RV Rentals." The yellow page directory online is also a resource where you might find local RV dealers who have rental units. A growing number of campgrounds offer on-site rentals too.

Before renting, read the agreement. Find out about charges that are over and above the basic rental fee. If insurance is not included, check with your auto insurer first to see if you will be covered in the rented vehicle. You may not need the insurance offered by the rental company. For most RV rentals you'll be responsible to pay for fuel and oil and per-mile charges. Do a price comparison with two or three rental companies to ensure you're getting the best value.

Once you decide on the dates for your trip in the rental unit, plan the route, stop at different types of campgrounds and RV parks along the way. Use the rig for more than a week to actually experience living on board. Learn the routines of driving, fueling, going into campsites, hooking up and breaking camp and dumping the tanks. Stay more than a couple days at one place and give yourself a chance to experience day-to-day routines of living in an RV. Cook some meals in the rig, enjoy your campsite and use the amenities at the RV park. Don't be too ambitious about the distance you plan to drive each day. Remember, you want to begin to experience the RV lifestyle, and it's a laid-back, relaxing one!

Online Resources

For Sale: New & Used RVs

www.rvusa.com
RV Marketplace for buyers, sellers and owners.

www.rvonline.com
Features new and used RVs for sale

www.RVTrader.com
Large inventory; multiple search options.

RV Rentals

www.cruiseamerica.com
The largest RV rental company in the United States.

www.elmonterv.com
Based in California, has locations throughout the U.S.

Used RV Prices

www.nadaguides.com
Click on *Recreation Vehicles* to get values for used RVs.

Did you know...

As early as 1920, travelers often "camped" in a simple wooden structure that they built in their backyard and then mounted on a Model T chassis to recreate their home environment on the road.

Chapter 7

Two Homes: Snow Birds & Part-Timers

"Dare to live the life you have dreamed for yourself.
Go forward and make your dreams come true."
— *Ralph Waldo Emerson*

Even though you have a land-locked domicile, if you will be gone from it for extended periods of time in the RV, there are certain aspects of day-to-day life you will need to adjust. But – thanks to cell phones, lap top computers, tablets and other electronic communication marvels – you can have just about all the comforts and conveniences of home in your home on wheels. Here are some things you'll want to set up before you leave for a month or more:

Mail

Do not let mail accumulate at your home for an extended period of time. It's an open invitation to thieves. If you are a snow bird who will be at a single location for more than a month, find out how to send mail to yourself at the RV park where you'll be staying. Then submit an official change of address form. Do it online or at the local post office a couple of weeks before you plan to leave. On the form, clearly indicate this is a temporary move, and be sure to list the date when you want the mail to stop going to your temporary location. Leaving that date off the form is a common mistake, and causes the post office system to default to one year (a default that's very difficult to change). A few weeks before you plan to return home, submit another change of address form to get a change from the snow bird location back to your home, effectively reversing the mail delivery process. There is no charge for this service.

If you plan to be away for a shorter period of time, less than 30 consecutive days, complete a stop delivery form, either on line or in person at your local post office. If you will be moving from place to place for longer than 30 days, have a relative, friend or neighbor get your mail daily and hold it till you return home. With most personal business being done electronically these days, snail mail delivery is no longer a critical issue.

If you experience any problems with USPS mail service, call toll free 800-ASK-USPS (275-9777).

Home Maintenance

If you will be gone during summer months, arrange for yard maintenance and lawn mowing, if applicable. And if winter is your time to be away from the site-built house, arrange for snow shoveling service and ice removal when needed. Also, be sure to leave an emergency contact with your home security system provider in case the alarm gets tripped. Someone nearby, preferably a trusted nearby neighbor, should have a key for use in an emergency. That neighbor should also have the name and phone number of a relative or close friend in the area who will be able to handle any emergency situation that might arise.

Finances / The Bills

Thanks to electronic communications, much of the manual paperwork associated with periodic financial transactions has been eliminated. If you haven't already done so, be sure all your income payments are being deposited to your bank account electronically. There's no need to receive paper checks that require your running to the bank to deposit them. Electronic deposits are not only easier, they are safer. Monthly bills: mortgage, other loans, utilities, credit cards, etc. can also be paid electronically, or by using online banking.

Vehicle Registrations and Insurance

Don't forget to take the registration and proof of insurance documentation for the RV as well as the dinghy or tow vehicle.

Medical Insurance and Prescription Drugs

Check the particulars of your medical insurance coverage to be sure you'll be able to use medical facilities in other states in an emergency. Medicare is OK to use anywhere. Most secondary (Medicare supplement) carriers, including the HMOs, also have provisions and procedures for medical care when you are away from home. Know the procedures just in case you need medical care on the road.

Have your prescriptions filled at a pharmacy that has a nationwide network. Both Walgreens and Walmart pharmacies have good systems with locations all over the country. Once your prescription is on their computer (and it's been authorized for by your physician), you can get it renewed anywhere in the country.

Staying Connected

Three areas where you'll want to be electronically connected from your RV are: Phone, Internet and TV.

Phones

If you don't already have a wireless phone, get one (or two) before you go on the road. Nowadays, smartphones offer voice, messaging and data options. The phone enables you to stay in touch with family and friends, make campground reservations and take care of other personal business from your home on wheels. And, obviously, the smartphone in your purse or pocket is invaluable in case of emergency. More detailed phone information can be found in Chapter 8: "Full-Timing"

Internet

There are basically three ways to get onto the Internet while on the road:

1) Your cellular phone service can be the gateway to high speed data connections for the Wi-Fi-enabled devices you have onboard, such as tablets, lap top computers and printers.

2) Wi-Fi "hot spot" technology may be available at some campgrounds, RV parks and public places, such as libraries and coffee shops. In hot

spot areas many users can share unsecured Wi-Fi networks. Some are free, others charge for use.

3) Internet service is available via satellite if you have a satellite dish at your rig.

TV

Most RVs are furnished with a TV or two. In populated areas, you will be able to pick up local channels at no additional cost. Cable TV plug-in access is usually available at RV park sites, and generally the charge for this service is included in the basic camping fee. You can also get extensive TV programming via satellite by adding a dish (rooftop or manual on a tripod) to your rig and subscribing to the service with one of two major carriers.

Note: More details about staying connected and online resources for electronic communications can be found in the next chapter.

Pack For An Extended Time Away

The RV is your home as you roam. Pack all the household items you'll need in the kitchen/dining area and stock the pantry and fridge. Make up the bed and take extra linens and towels. Place your clothing into closets and drawers. Remember that everything you pack will be in motion as you travel, which means they'll be shifting around, so you'll want to take things in plastic bottles (no glass!) and dishes and cooking utensils should be non-breakable. Bring those special items that make your house a home, like family photos and grandma's afghan. But remove the photos from the frames and leave the glass behind.

An RVer should not be without essential tools on the road. See the toolbox checklist included in Chapter 10.

The Pet(s)

Last, but not least, don't forget about Fido or Fluffy. Many RVers do travel with pets. They are not only important members of the family but excellent traveling companions. For the most part, pets are allowed at campgrounds, with reasonable restrictions. Very few campgrounds prohibit pets, and there are a handful that don't allow very large dogs (like Saint Bernards)…although I wonder why anyone would consider traveling with very large dogs anyway. It seems unkind to the dogs to have them crammed into restrictive quarters on a daily basis. The living area of an RV lends itself to small pets.

Now for the reasonable restrictions at RV parks:

- Pets (including cats) must always be on a leash when outside the RV.
- The pooper-scooper rule is strictly enforced.
- Excessive barking is not allowed.

Before taking a dog on the road ask yourself, is my dog a good camper? A dog that's a good camper doesn't bark every time someone walks past the campsite, and doesn't bark incessantly when left alone in the RV for a few hours. People live in relatively close quarters at campgrounds. Does your dog's temperament and disposition lend itself to the RV lifestyle? If you're not sure, you will find out soon enough. Picture this, you just pulled into an RV park near Chicago and you decide to take the train into the city to go on a six-hour guided tour of the city. Dogs aren't allowed on trains or buses, so the pet stays home. When you get back to the campground that evening, tired after a hard day of sightseeing, you're asked to leave. "Pull out now," the man says. Evicted! Wow, that never happened to you before. Turns out you picked a campground with zero tolerance for incessantly barking dogs, and yours barked continuously for eight straight hours. The campground owner took complaints all day and was at his wits end by the time you arrived back home.

It goes without saying, if your dog has a tendency to bite, you might want to reconsider taking him on the road. However, most dogs we've met in our travels are friendly and good campers. We've observed it's because their owners are willing to give them the attention they require, thus the pets happily adapt to acceptable camping routines. Most pets enjoy the traveling as much as their owners do.

A final reminder, be sure your pet's inoculations are up to date and bring the documentation along.

Online Resources

Mail Service

www.usps.gov

Click on change of address to get mail sent to your temporary location, or Click on hold mail if you will be away for less than 30 days.

Prescription Drugs

www.cvs.com

Over 7,600 stores nationwide. Store locator feature on website.

www.walgreens.com

Over 8,000 stores nationwide. Store locator feature on website.

www.walmart.com

Over 4,000 stores nationwide. Store locator feature on website.

RV Lifestyle

www.rversonline.org

Over 2,000 pages of non-commercial RV-related information based on the premise of RVers-helping-RVers. No advertising on this site. Also has a Facebook page.

Chapter 8

Full-Timing: The Home Base and More

"Home is where we park it."
— *The Full-Timers Mantra*

Hopefully, so far, this book has given you enough useful information so you can make an educated decision about full-timing. If you decide to adopt the full-time RV lifestyle, this chapter will be of particular interest and value. Every full-timing situation is as unique as the people involved, but certain issues apply to all. At the end of this chapter, you'll find a handy check list for making the transition to full-timing as well as a listing of resources you may want to use.

First step: sell the house or vacate the apartment! Once you make the decision to go full-timing, this is the starting point. When we tell people we're full-timers, invariably we will get questions like: Did you sell the house or buy the RV first? What did you do with all your stuff? Where do you get your mail? How do you pay your bills? Don't you feel insecure without a home? Where do you spend most of your time? Don't you ever get tired of traveling? This chapter is designed to answer these questions and more.

I'll begin at the beginning. Here's the schedule we established as a framework to transition to full-timing (not necessarily in the order listed):

- Put the house and business on the market simultaneously.

- Buy an RV.

- Send lists of furniture and other items to the family, asking what they want. (We took two trips up north in a rented truck and delivered about half our furniture and other household items to family. The rest, we sold locally or donated to the Salvation Army.)

- Decide on a home base and do the required paperwork to establish a new address.

- Rent a shed to hold enough furniture to get us started in case we decide after a year we want to go back to stick-house living.

Together, these specific tasks formed a plan of action that we accomplished during an 11-month period. It is suggested that you outline your own general plan of action…one that's tailored to your specific situation. What worked for us may not work for you. For instance, you may be planning to rent out your house rather than sell it. Some full-timers do this in order to provide a stream of income while they're on the road. Before you create a rental unit, though, consider the problems that come with being an absentee landlord. You might already own an RV, so you won't need to factor the purchase into your plan, or you may not need to get a place to store stuff. The one item on the "transition-to-full-time" plan that can't be eliminated or ignored is establishing a home state.

Choose A Home State

Every full-time traveler must have a home base – a home address, usually a mail box somewhere in the state of your choice. So, pick a state! Here's where you have an advantage over the people with land-locked domiciles. You can select the state that is most beneficial to you. The key factors to consider are:

- State income tax
- State sales tax
- Personal property tax
- Vehicle licensing and registration
- Requirements for safety and emissions testing
- Personal preferences

Taxes are a fact of life. We all pay federal taxes, but state income, sales and personal property taxes vary widely, as do vehicle registration and licensing costs.

The three most popular home base states for full-timers are Florida, Texas and South Dakota. None has a state income tax. South Dakota has a low sales tax and is also popular because it has many mail forwarding services that cater to full-timers. Montana has no sales tax and is used by many for vehicle registration. There are a few other states with no state income tax that can be considered.

Texas is home to the Escapees Club, a big club that includes many full-time RVers. It has a good mail forwarding service. For many, this is one of the reasons to home base in Texas. Both Texas and Florida are popular snow bird destinations, attracting many full-timers who would be going there anyway for a couple of winter months. Having a sun belt state as a home base makes it convenient to schedule annual tasks where consistency is desirable, such as medical checkups, tax preparations and other personal business.

Choosing a home base state is an important decision. Simply selecting a state that has low or no state income tax is not always the best option. Other issues, such as vehicle registration, emissions testing, inheritance tax and community property law may need to be considered. A guide book entitled "Choosing Your RV Home Base" contains detailed and useful information you'll need to make state-by-state comparisons. It can short-cut the research process and help you decide which state can best suit your individual needs. The book is listed in the "Resources" section at the end of this chapter.

Mail

In most states, you must meet the requirement of having a physical address as your domicile. Property ownership is not required – just a street address. After you select a state, find a location you can claim as an address. This new street address is where you'll receive your mail, so pick a place that has dependable mail forwarding service. When you go into your new home state to rent a mailbox and arrange for mail forwarding services, you can obtain vehicle registrations, drivers licenses and voter registration at the same time. Be sure your new address is the street address and the number sign (#). For example, 543 Main St., #113 (Apt. 113 is also acceptable). But do not use the "PMB" designation (which stands for Personal or Private Mailbox). "PMB" is not required by the post office, so all it does is to send up a red flag signal that your domicile is a mailbox.

In our case, we were already living in Florida when we decided to become full-timers. Even if we hadn't already been Florida residents, we probably still would have selected it as our home base because taxes and registrations are reasonable and it is an attractive sun belt state. Our street address was at a franchised mail store. In the winter, when in Florida for a month or so, we'd stop at our home address to pick up mail and say hi to the folks who have been forwarding our mail all over the country for the past year.

When shopping around for a mail forwarding service, look for a well-established and reliable business. We know people who rented a box at a mail store that had just opened. The owners promised excellent forwarding service, and they did give good service for about six months. Then one day the RVer called in for a mail forward only to find out the phone had been disconnected. The new mail store went out of business and never notified the traveling RVers.

Renting a box at the post office is not suitable for full-timers. In most states a P.O. box doesn't meet the address requirement. Also, the post office does not provide the kind of "call in" service that full-time travelers require. We need to have persons in the mail center who will be available to take down a different address every time we call in to have our mail forwarded.

Use the Internet to research mail forwarding services for RVers, and seek out recommendations from full-timers who are already using such a service.

Be consistent. Maintain one address where you'll receive your mail, register your vehicles, get your drivers license and register to vote. Change your address on everything you normally want to receive by mail. Monthly statements from credit cards and banks usually include a section for an address change. Don't forget about important mail you might get just once or twice a year (from life insurance, financial institutions, etc.). Many organizations will accept address changes on line.

Your Permanent, Movable Home

Never again will you drive off and after a while say, "Oh no, I left my running shoes, or my jacket (or some other item) at home." You ARE at home. Nothing to forget, nothing to worry about back there. What an incredible sense of freedom full-time RVers experience!

Here are a couple of simple guidelines to follow when loading up the rig:

- Avoid anything glass. Don't bring your favorite stemware or breakable dinnerware. You can say you'll be careful, but your home is a moving vehicle and the day is apt to come when you forget to secure a cabinet door; then you'll have a huge clean-up job on your hands. Those precious family pictures may look great on the walls or atop the dresser, but if you want to bring them along in the RV, ditch the frames and especially the glass.

- Use the three-quarters rule to determine what you'll take. That is, take only enough items to fill about 75% of the total space of your cabinets, drawers and storage bins. That will leave an empty cabinet or drawer or bin in various parts of the RV. Never fear, you'll accumulate more "stuff" soon enough. But, over time, you will also learn the art of getting by with only what you need.

- Pack tight. When packing the storage bins underneath and cabinets inside the rig, pack tight. Items shift around when the rig is moving. It's better to have one storage bin packed tight and another totally empty rather then having two packed half full. Store heavy items toward the floor or bottom of the rig. Lighter items should be in upper cabinets. For dishes and cups in kitchen cabinets, use non-skid shelf liners to prevent items from sliding around.

Banking / Finances

If you're satisfied with your current bank, but plan to establish a home base in another state, you don't necessarily have to switch to a bank in the new state or to one of the larger multi-state banks. When was the last time you had to go inside the bank to take care of business? Most recurring transactions nowadays are electronic, and this process will continue uninterrupted when you go on the road. All you have to do is send the bank a change of address. Online banking continues uninterrupted after you hit the road. Concerned about the bill payments exceeding the money in the account occasionally? Most banks offer some form of overdraft protection.

Staying in touch from the road is easy these days.

Digital communications from the RV

Smartphones

For full-timers, the cellular phone is the home phone and the only phone number(s) you have. When the land line gets disconnected give the cell phone number as the new number on the recorded message that runs for 30 days afterward. Wireless phone service is available throughout the country, and since you'll be traveling to many area codes, you will want to use a company with consistent nationwide service – currently AT&T Wireless and Verizon are regarded as the carriers with best overall coverage. Both have retail and online stores where you can consult with a technician to set up a plan for your unique RVing needs and budget. Use the store locator feature on the company's website to find a location where you can actually go in and meet personally with a technician to design your cellular plan. NOTE: Be sure to verify that it is a company-owned store, as that's where you will find the knowledgeable service personnel.

Wireless Data Service

There are three major ways you can connect to the Internet while traveling: Cellular, Satellite or Wi-Fi hot spots.

Cellular: The cellular phone system has become so extensive that it is now a reliable option for full Internet access on the road. The two largest carriers offer the most contiguous coverage. You can access the Internet directly on a smartphone or tether your phone to the computer to establish a connection. Another way to use cellular for Internet access is a Wi-Fi hot spot. A smartphone can act as Wi-Fi hot spots, or you could get a Mobile Hot Spot battery powered modem. AT&T's MiFi Liberate or Verizon's MiFi Jetpack can handle up to 10 Wi-Fi-enabled devices at 4G LTE speed. Consult with your carrier for technical advice and to get a data plan to fit your level of usage and budget. Data security with cellular devices is very good, and cellular is the only technology that allows you to be connected while traveling down the road.

Satellite: This is the technology that works virtually everywhere as long as the satellite dish has an unobstructed view of the southern sky (don't park under a tree). However, there are longer delays with a satellite Internet connection, and it is the most expensive of the three methods listed here.

Wi-Fi Hot Spots: Networks are installed at many campgrounds and public Wi-Fi hot spots can also be found at libraries and coffee shops. Some are free and some charge a user fee. When you are using a hot spot, you are sharing the Internet service at that location with other users, so data security of e-mail communications can be an issue. When using a shared network you need to be within range of the host.

TV In The RV

Nearly every RV has a TV (or two) as part of the standard furnishings. All you need to do is decide what type of TV service you'll use. If you add a satellite dish—there are two basic styles: push-button rooftop or manual on a tripod—you can subscribe to the hundreds of channels available through one of two major satellite TV companies. The company provides the receiver (as well as the monthly bill). If you don't want to invest in the satellite equipment, most campgrounds have a cable TV hookup at the site and it's generally included in the camping fee. You will also be able to get local channels in most locations free.

You Too Can Be A Savvy Digital Consumer

The preceding section contains a brief, bare-bones outline of the electronic communications currently available for today's RVers. Just 20 years ago, they wouldn't have been possible. If you are "technically challenged," like I am, you might be somewhat overwhelmed by this section. Today's retirees did not grow up in the digital age...the bits, bytes, kilobytes, and so on seem like a foreign language to us. When I purchased my first "smart" phone, I quickly discovered that I wasn't "smart" enough to teach myself how to use it, and my 11-year-old granddaughter, Megan, became my best teacher.

Before you decide which electronic devices you want to have onboard your RV, gather information, troll the RV forums for facts and opinions, use the Internet resources listed at the end of this chapter and ask other RVers about the communications they use. Before you purchase electronic equipment and digital devices, discuss your situation with a technician. Ask a lot of questions. We found that the younger techs usually have a better grasp of digital electronics. You're not going to become a geek overnight, but you definitely need to determine which electronic devices will suit your needs and budget. Do your research and become an educated consumer who will ultimately make wise decisions.

Important Papers and Valuables

Our house on wheels doesn't have a security system like our stick-built house did. Although the RV is reasonably safe and secure whether on the road or parked, accidents do happen. A concern we had about being on the road full time was that our children would have access to information they would need in the event of a common disaster. Important papers are not as secure traveling around in an RV as they would be, for instance, in a stationary metal box on the shelf of the bedroom closet. Our solution was to rent a bank safe deposit box for storing important papers and valuables. Another option is to place the important papers in a fire-proof metal box and leave them with a family member or trusted friend. Either way, the originals of your vital documents won't be at risk by dragging them all over the country. You may also want to consider placing valuable jewelry in the safe box.

Before going on the road we sorted through and carefully organized all our financial records and important papers. This was another good result that came out of the preparations to go full-time. Organizing and updating records is a chore people tend to put off...and we're no different. Plowing through all the paper, we found duplicates and outdated stuff that could be put through the shredder. When the tasks were finished, we had a well-organized stack of vital records including: wills and durable powers of attorney, life insurance and annuity contracts, birth and marriage certificates, cemetery deed, stock certificates, savings bonds, documentation of current accounts and their financial institutions, property deed and military records. Most are now in the safe deposit box.

However, there are certain documents you'll need to keep in the RV or in the car. These include vehicle registrations and insurance documentation for both the motor home and dinghy or the truck and trailer. Also, we carry our passports in case we decide to go out of the country...and we have the vehicle titles with us in case we decide to replace either vehicle. These important originals are kept in the rig in a small fireproof box.

If you have a computer on board, you may want to scan all your important papers and burn the copies to a CD. It is a time-consuming process the first time, but updates (where applicable) won't take as long. There are software packages available to help you manage this process.

Medical Care and Prescription Drugs

Medical care and medical insurance coverage is always an important issue, but it takes on added significance as we move into retirement years. We've learned, since going on the road, that every individual is responsible to know all about their health records and be fully apprised of any medical conditions. Furthermore, we are responsible to keep ourselves in good shape – physically and mentally. In the long run, that's the best medical care.

Before you hit the road, have a general physical checkup from your current physician and, while you're there, ask for copies of all relevant medical records. It's a good idea to carry these documents with you. However, even though we've had several occasions when we needed to get emergency treatment at hospital emergency rooms and routine consultations at doctor's offices or walk-in clinics, not once did they ask for medical records. The first thing they want is proof of insurance. In one place I offered to bring my medical records and was told they prefer to do their own testing and diagnosis because health conditions change. And that made sense. However, they always asked for a record of all medications we're currently taking and, of course, proof of insurance.

This segues to the next topic: prescription drugs. If you have not already done so, take the time to make a list of all medications and doses (including vitamins) that you currently take. It is a sure sign of aging when you need to buy one of those little plastic boxes with S-M-T-W-T-F-S on top. You know the ones I'm talking about…the box that, in my younger days, I said I'd never need. Well, I need it now! The list of my medications and doses is taped to the inside cover of the plastic box, just to be sure I don't misplace the list.

Before you leave your land-locked domicile, have your prescriptions filled at a pharmacy that has a nationwide network. Once you're in their computer system you'll be able to have prescriptions filled with ease anywhere in the country. Check the number of refills the prescribing physician has authorized. Often the prescription is only good for 6 or 12 refills and then the doctor wants to see you to monitor whether you still need that medication and at that dosage. If and when this occurs you would need to decide whether you want to return to your previous doctor for an annual checkup, or find another doctor for a periodic checkup.

What if a problem arises and one of us needs to have surgery or go into a hospital for some other inpatient treatment? Believe it or not, living full-time in an RV is advantageous in such a situation. Have you ever seen a motor home or fifth wheel parked in a hospital lot with the jacks down? It's likely that an individual is in the hospital and the spouse is staying in the lot. Or, when the hospital stay is longer than a few days the spouse could pull into a nearby campground and hookup for the duration of the hospitalization.

Check your medical insurance plan(s) to determine procedures to be followed for obtaining routine medical care and in emergency situations. Most insurers (including Medicare) will honor claims from participating providers throughout the country. However, if you are in an HMO, their procedures can vary; call the carrier, explain your situation and ask for advice. It is possible that you might need to change insurers when you become a full-time traveler. It's better to confirm up front that your coverage will be valid rather than find out later when you file a claim after you're on the road.

Staying Healthy on the Road

Every RVer should have good knowledge of First Aid. If you've never taken a basic First Aid course, now is the time to do it. After all, you're retired. Call the local YMCA, health department at city hall or the community school and find out where you can enroll. First Aid and basic CPR courses are offered at some RV rallies. First Aid kit items should always be in your RV's medicine cabinet.

We're often asked, "At what age will you have to stop full-timing?" Age is not the major factor, health is! Maintain healthy routines to keep yourself in good shape. Exercise regularly, and eat sensibly.

There is no good reason to avoid exercise on the road. You may not be able to keep up your membership at the gym and the RV doesn't have room for a treadmill, but you can walk every day, everywhere you go…and walking is an effective form of exercise. RVers get to walk in varied locales, giving them a chance to see and appreciate each region's unique beauty. Other kinds of exercise for RVers include cycling, dancing, swimming, tennis and golf. My husband is a golf nut…he's enjoyed the experience of different courses all over the country and has had the pleasure of meeting locals wherever we go.

Walking is great sport. You never know when a walk will lead to a memorable experience. One time we were staying at a state park in Mississippi during off season. The weather was beautiful – mild, but not too hot – so I went on a long walk every day. A snow white beach on the Gulf was just across the street and there were woodsy areas around the park, so I was able to enjoy exploring both areas. One day I saw a path into the woods; a small wooden sign read "outdoor chapel." Out of curiosity I followed the path for half a mile or so when it opened on to a clearing that had a small set of wooden benches facing a rough hewn wooden altar. The trees formed a cathedral ceiling over the area. I sat on the bench for a long time, savoring the silence. And, alone in that quiet, hushed clearing in the woods, I felt the presence of God. I will long remember the feeling of serenity that washed over me that day in the little outdoor chapel in the Mississippi woods.

RV Insurance

Some companies that insure RVs do not provide coverage for full-timers. But there are plenty of insurers that do. As a matter of fact, when you begin shopping for insurance, you'll find more than enough RV carriers to get comparative price quotes. However, it's important to declare yourself as a full-timer when you fill out the application for insurance. If you don't and have the misfortune to be in an accident where you need to submit a claim, you could be denied coverage. In addition to the usual motor vehicle coverage, it's advisable to get replacement value insurance for the RV.

Emergency road service is very important. Most RVers couldn't even handle the basic tire change on such a large vehicle. And towing an RV in for repairs is an expensive proposition. So, emergency road service is definitely necessary. Most motor home insurance policies can include emergency road service. RV clubs and associations also offer policies for road service. Compare coverage and prices from several companies and buy the policy that's most suitable for you.

Storage Unit

At the beginning, I was unsure whether I would even like the RV lifestyle, much less enjoy doing it full time. Everything was entirely new and totally unfamiliar. I learned RVing by immersion. Going RVing full-time was a leap of faith for me. So, we made a commitment to try it for a year and we prepared for the possibility that we'd go back to a land-locked domicile.

Initially, the purpose of renting a storage unit was to keep some furniture to get us started should we move back into a house next year. One year flowed into two and then three and we continued to pay rent on the climate controlled storage unit. At the beginning of the fourth year, I calculated how much we had spent for renting the storage shed versus the approximate value of the "stuff" we had stored there. It was no longer worth it…especially now that my perspective had changed.

Material possessions are not that important anymore. A whole house full of beautiful furniture will never be as lovely as walking in the Redwood Forest…a wide screen TV will never be as spectacular as the sunset over the desert…having my own swimming pool would not ever compare to wading into the Pacific and Atlantic Oceans, the Gulf of Mexico, Lake Michigan and the Mississippi River all in the same year (not in that order). You'll not fully appreciate the spectacular natural beauty of this country by flying over it, nor will you appreciate all this country has to offer during quick two-week trips in the car. When I saw the Grand Canyon for the first time, I thought, "Now I've seen the most wondrous of my country's natural wonders." But that was just the beginning. Since then, I've been fortunate enough to see dozens more natural wonders. There has been so much more to see, savor and appreciate! Every day is a beautiful day of discovery.

After looking inside the storage unit, we wondered why in the world we kept all that stuff, and then proceeded to give it all away, including fairly new TVs that went to some nice young people. We got a lot more joy from the giving than they did from the getting.

For the irreplaceable items such as family photos and heirlooms a small climate controlled storage unit, about the size of a large walk-in closet, works…and the cost is modest. Another option is to give those things to family members who are apt to inherit them someday anyway. At least you'll be around to see the treasured items being used.

The Choice Includes Some Trade-Offs

After being a full-time RVer for many years, members of my family, to a person, still cannot understand nomadic life. No one in the family has ever done RV-type traveling. So the lifestyle is as foreign to them, as it was to me when I first moved into our wonderful motor home. My brother still jokingly asks if I've yet decided what I want to do when I grow up. The grandchildren (when we're parked in a campground near their home) enjoyed coming to visit the RV. They get a kick out of Granny's house on wheels; it looks like a great big play house. Their parents, on the other hand, were somewhat apprehensive.

Full-time RVing is a lifestyle that traditionalists don't understand. When we sang "Over the river and through the woods, to grandmother's house we go," we weren't singing about grandmother's house on wheels. When grandmother is traveling all the time, she's viewed as a "gypsy," surely not as the grandma in an apron whose kitchen always has the delicious aroma of fresh-baked apple pie.

In some ways, full-timers suffer from trailer-park-trash stigma, no matter what the price tag on the rig was. Full-timing is incredibly rewarding, and can take us to the happiest of the retirement years, but there are trade-offs. Full-time RVing grandparents do not have the pleasure of children and grandchildren "coming home" to visit for holidays or to be gathered around the dining room table for Sunday dinner. Some RVing grandparents are lucky enough to have grandchildren travel with them occasionally. But for many others, whose families want to keep their distance from the "strange" lifestyle, it's just a dream that will never come true.

While the RV affords full-timers a way to see friends and family frequently, they are always the traveling visiting relatives and rarely have the pleasure of hosting visitors at their home. Some view this as a disadvantage. However, full-time RVing is still the best way for a couple of adventurous old(er) folks to spend part or all of their retirement years. The joy is in the journey!

You Can Go Home Again

When thinking about full-time RVing for retirement, most people instinctively know the day will come when they have to hang up the keys...and they worry about it. "Isn't it better to buy a small place now to have for the future?" they ask. Well sure, if you want to pay property taxes, utilities and maintenance on an empty place for however long you're on the road. (Refer back to Chapter 3.) Another approach might be to earmark part of the nest egg for future use and let it gain a reasonable rate of return during your full-timing years. Put the house in the bank, so to speak. Land-locked properties will always be on the market. Meanwhile you can enjoy freedom to explore all the states in this great land. And, if and when you're ready, you'll have a better idea of the next place you want to call home.

Full-Timers Checklist

❏ Shop and research thoroughly before buying an RV.

❏ Sell the house.

❏ Decide what to do with furnishings and other "stuff" & disburse them.

❏ Rent storage unit if needed.

◻ Obtain insurance to cover the RV for full-time living.

◻ Prepare & pack the rig.

◻ Pick a home state; establish the new address.

◻ Change address on everything normally received in the mail.

◻ Review financial records & important papers.

◻ Decide where to store important papers & valuables.

◻ Arrange to have financial transactions done electronically.

◻ Confirm that current health insurance will cover full time travelers.

◻ Disconnect phone land line; use cell phone number as forward.

◻ Transition from desktop to laptop computer.

◻ Have medical checkup & get relevant medical records.

◻ Get current/new prescription(s).

◻ Arrange to have prescription(s) filled at national pharmacy.

◻ Make list of medications.

◻ Get pet's shots updated & obtain relevant records from vet.

Online Resources

Insurance

www.explorerrv.com
Specializes in coverage for RVs, full-time & part-time.

www.rvainsurance.com
RV America offers comparative RV insurance quotes.

Mail Service

www.escapees.com/MailForwardingService/HowToApply.asp
Mail forwarding service of the Escapees RV Club.

www.fmca.com
Mail forwarding service from Family Motor Coach Association.

Road Service Plans

www.coachnet.com
Knowledgeable and timely emergency service specifically for RVs

www.goodsamroadside.com
Emergency Road Service sponsored by Good Sam RV Club.

Satellite Equipment

www.kvh.com
Mobile satellite systems for TV and Internet

www.winegard.com
Satellite dish antennas, roof-mounted and portable.

www.kingcontrols.com
Satellite TV dish antennas and accessories

Satellite Internet Provider

www.hughesnet.com
Full Internet access through a satellite modem to your computer. Largest provider.

Satellite TV Providers

www.dish.com
Primary satellite TV provider - entertainment, sports, movies, many channels. Also can provide Internet service.

www.directtv.com
Many TV channels via satellite, full programming sports and entertainment. Also has Internet service.

Selecting A Home State

www.travelbooksusa.com
Choosing Your RV Home Base, paperback guide outlines how to pick a home state. Also available at Amazon.com

Smartphones & Internet Connections

www.att.com/wireless
www.verizonwireless.com

Two largest nationwide carriers for products, service and technical support. Cell phones and Internet connections. Shop at company-owned stores or online.

Vehicle License & Registration

www.dmv.org
Nationwide Departments of Motor Vehicles state-by-state guide.

www.usa.gov/Topics/Motor-Vehicles.shtml
Links for all 50 states to get or renew your driver's license, register your vehicle, or other motor vehicle services.

Did you know...

The average RVing couple carries approximately 2,000 pounds of "stuff," while the average full-time couple carries about 3,000 pounds.

Chapter 9

On The Road

"On the road again,
Just can't wait to get on the road again..."
— Willie Nelson

Do It Your Way

Go where you want, stay where you want, for as long as you want. That about sums it up. When you go RVing, you are in the driver's seat, literally and figuratively. The big day finally arrives, all the arrangements have been made and the trip is about to begin. So, how is it done?

The best answer is: do it your way...develop your own one-of-a-kind RV travel model as you go along. The RV lifestyle is learned only by actually doing it on the road.

Our first trip in the RV – the maiden voyage, so to speak – was going to be just a two-week jaunt within our home state, from Jacksonville to Key West, with one or perhaps two stops along the way.

I was hell-bent on a true nomadic existence. "Should we make reservations?" asked my husband, the driver, the night before we left.

"Don't be silly," said I, the co-pilot, (who, by the way, had no previous camping experience). "We'll find places to stay along the way." Well-armed with two huge campground directories (it was the "old days," before digital listings) I was confident. We drove for a few hours when I finally decided to crack open the brand new giant campground book. For a newbie, it was overwhelming! All those little marks on the map. Where are we now? What's the milepost? Where will we be when it's time to stop for the night? There was so much to cross reference, from the map to the listings...back 'n forth, back 'n forth. Before long I was taking notes furiously. Cities along the route, current milepost, milepost an hour from now.

Then I started with the questions: How many amps do we need? What's a central dump? Is typical site width 30' good for us? Are we a big rig? Why do they say heaters allowed?

Finally, my driver (the experienced but exasperated camper) said, "Enough already! Just pick something, I'm tired!" I selected one listing and phoned them; yes, we have a couple of spots for tonight, just give us your name and credit card number. Armed with the hefty directory, I directed us to the campground, and thus successfully carried out my first co-pilot chore.

But, when we arrived, were we ever surprised! It was a classic "trailer park" – mostly permanent residents, and a couple of spaces near the back of the property for the rare overnighter who, like us, happened to venture in off the road. It seemed like every one of the residents came out of their trailers to watch us get our brand new rig settled into the spot next to the back fence. I tried to ignore the audience. "I'm tired, I don't care," muttered the driver as he plugged in the electric and hooked up the water. I'd like to say we had a restful first night in our new home, but we were backed into a site at the rear end of the property where only a chain link fence separated us from the railroad tracks. At least three freight trains whistled through during the night.

The next morning, we weight-lifted both campground directories onto the table, figured out how to navigate through them and made a few phone calls to south Florida. It was January, the height of the season in the south. We were able to find available space in the Keys, but just barely. We secured two nights at one RV park and three at another. And the nightly fees were much higher than we expected. So much for the anticipated week at the beach.

The first trip, our test run, wasn't a rousing success, but we sure did learn a lot. Even nomads have to be sensible, especially when they're in a 38-foot motor home with a toad. That behemoth can't randomly pull over and stay just anywhere for the night.

But, this is RVing…an adventure. After those first few days we were well on the way toward developing our own personal RV style. The major attraction to the RV experience is that it gives adventurous travelers a way to explore new places, soak up the unique environs of different parts of the country and meet the people who reflect the personality of the region. As retirees, you can go RVing state by state, region by region or destination to destination at your own pace.

In spite of the inauspicious beginning, we two happily traveled full-time for many years and developed a travel style that's comfortable and fun for us.

In our travels we've observed that RV travel styles can range from free spirit to groupies, and everything in between. But most people are a little of both styles.

"Free spirits" are classic happy wanderers, not too regimented. They enjoy being with people, but they also want to go off into the wilderness to enjoy hiking, fishing and just being with nature. Then they'll decide to go to a major city they've not seen before and take a guided tour. Generally the free spirits don't set schedules too far in advance. They are the ones who drive the family "back home" crazy. Usually, when free spirits call family, the first question is, "Where are you now?" Conversely, "groupies" join clubs, attend monthly group camp-outs and like to plan and arrange RV club events. Very often they become club officers and actively recruit new members. They get involved in activities such as Volunteers on Wheels and Habitat for Humanity. Groupies like to travel in caravans. Some also supplement their incomes by leading caravans or by selling their wares at RV rallies. Unlike the free spirits, their schedules are set well in advance.

There is no specific plan of action for RV traveling. Traveling styles are as unique as the individuals and their rigs. Here are a few points (not necessarily in any logical order) that have enhanced our travel experiences:

- An informational stop per state. Whenever we cross a state line, we stop at the Welcome Center. There's a plethora of valuable information to be had at these places. Browsing the brochures will give you a feel for the personality of the state. Some travelers look specifically for museums, others zero in on historic sites, entertainment venues, tourist attractions, outdoor activities or state and federal parks. If you don't see what you're looking for, ask. Some centers file information about their state and county parks under the counter. Welcome Centers are a good resource for travelers and some of them even offer coffee and cookies.

- Don't push and tire yourself out. After a few weeks, you'll have enough experience to be able to establish a general guideline for how many hours/miles per day are suitable for you. Everyone has their own comfort level. Keep reminding yourself that you're retired now…no longer on the job; it will take some time to wind down.

- Be flexible. Our friends Carla and Skip started counting the days a full year before they retired. They were going to be extended travelers – not quite full-timing, but leaving their land-locked domicile behind for months at a time to go out and play. By the time the big day arrived, they had their first journey—three months in duration—thoroughly scheduled. About a week after they left, both came down with the flu. They were in Arkansas and had to hunker down at a campground for a few days longer than the one night that was on the carefully-crafted schedule. "My whole schedule is shot," Skip reported to us. "I had to make a dozen phone calls to cancel reservations along the way, and then figure out how we're going to make up the lost time."

  After we got that call from Skip, I thought about it. Did our friends really have to make up for "lost time?" It reminded me that, at our age, there is no such thing as "lost" time, just "more" time…time given to appreciate and enjoy being retired, even if it's a few extra nights in Arkansas sipping chicken soup.

- Avoid driving at night. Once we were driving on a main road in a remote part of the great state of Texas. It was getting to be mid-afternoon when I queried, "It looks like there's a nice campground coming up in a few miles. Want to stop there for tonight?" The pilot wasn't tired and felt like going another 50 miles or so. We breezed by the nice campground, not realizing it would be the last one for about 200 miles. It was dark, pitch black, when we finally pulled in for the night, tired and cranky. Another lesson learned. Remote areas can be tricky when it comes to finding places to stay. Stopping well before sunset is better than driving into the dark.

- Always drive defensively. This can never be emphasized enough. Be aware of the other drivers on the road; give them plenty of room when they're passing. Don't make any sudden, sharp moves. Always be aware of the size of the vehicle you're driving and the space required to pass, to make turns or to cut across lanes of traffic. If you miss an exit, keep going. Above all, don't speed. Seeing an RV accident is a sobering experience and, the first time you see one, it will reinforce all the aforementioned tips.

- Avoid peak times and days. A recent study identified the 10 deadliest days on the roadways of America: Jan. 1, July 2, 3 & 4, Aug. 3, 4, 6 & 12, Sept. 2 and Dec. 23. These days are all associated with holidays and/or vacation times. The day before Thanksgiving is also a hazardous day on the roads. One of the benefits of being a traveling retiree is we can avoid the heavy traffic times and days. Don't go out on the roadways on days when it seems like the rest of the country is rushing to get somewhere for a holiday or a vacation. It is also wise to plan your drive times to steer clear of rush hours in major metropolitan areas.

- Watch the weather. Since we're on the road, the Weather Channel has become one of our favorite stations. Always check the weather on your travel route and in the general vicinity of your destination. Even though you wake up to a clear and sunny day, you could be surprised by inclement weather en route. Avoid high winds and driving in stormy weather. Keep yourselves informed about weather patterns. Remember, your home is on wheels. Consequently you're capable of outrunning a hurricane or getting out of the way of a tornado.

GPS (Global Positioning System)

GPS—the satellite-based navigational system—uses a network of 24 satellites in orbit to continuously transmit signal information to the earth. A GPS receiver uses that information to calculate the precise location of the receiver and create directions to any other location. This information is displayed on the GPS receiver's electronic map.

GPS is an essential navigation tool for RV travelers. It identifies your exact location (anywhere, at any given time) and it provides precise voice and on-screen directions from Point A to Point B; it can also give detour directions to avoid traffic problems, find the nearest gas stations, rest areas, shopping, restaurants, and much more. The places it can take you to are seemingly endless, as long as the coordinates, or even the street addresses, are in its data base.

Prices range from about $100 for an entry-level GPS to between $200-$400 for RV-specific devices. Cellular phones can be used as a GPS also. Generally, any GPS device can provide basic directions, but many go beyond the basics. RV-specific devices usually have a larger screen, the option to enter profile information for your rig (i.e., weight, height, length, etc.), an option to give the GPS verbal instructions rather than keying them in, identifies road hazards and, RV/truck routes and has detailed campground and RV park listings, locations of major attractions and landmarks and more.

Trip Planning

By now you probably have a general idea of where you want to go and the things you want to do once you hit the road. Planning the trip can be as exciting as taking the trip itself. Here are some key trip-planning tools:

- Free computerized map programs that will calculate routes (quickest, shortest, most scenic, etc.) to a destination or series of destinations. Rather than using the GPS for mapping, you may want to pull up one of those programs onto the lap top so you'll have the benefit of a wider screen as well as a note pad beside you as you consider different routes and destinations.

- RV travel books and Internet sites about specific areas of the country and popular destinations. You can find websites dedicated to everything from scenic drives to amenities along the interstates as well as places to find free overnight parking. Informative books geared specifically to campers are available to help you find a variety of places from national parks and state parks to casinos, factory tours, popular attractions and even the very-necessary dump stations. Purchasing a book that narrows the field to your particular interest can save you many frustrating hours of surfing the net. RV bookstores online and in specialty stores such as Camping World have the books for RV travelers.

- Traditional atlas—the big paperback one that's been a staple in every vehicle since 1954—is still being used. RV-copilots still want to have the state-by-state map in the lap. There are times in every traveler's day when they need to reach for a specialty book instead of an electronic device.

Places To Go / Things To See

One thing is certain about America The Beautiful – it's big! So much to see…so many great places to discover. The U.S. Interstate Highway System is unique – there's nothing like it in the world. Most of your RV driving will be done on the 46,000+ miles of efficient, generally well-maintained and mostly free interstates. And, at other times, you'll also get to experience the charm of other highways and byways.

Places waiting for you out there include:

- Public Lands
- The 49th State
- Historic Sites and Museums
- Cities, Towns and Waterways

Public Lands: Recreational activities abound at national parks and forests, along the nation's waterways and in the mountains. Camping on public lands puts you right where the action is! However, larger sites with hookups are not available in all areas, especially wilderness and forest preserves. Reservations for big rig campsites should be made well in advance, especially during peak tourist seasons. The 12 national parks that form the sweeping "grand circle" from Utah to Arizona and Colorado are especially popular, as are Yellowstone and Yosemite. Excellent camping, fishing and water sports can be found at Corps of Engineers-managed campgrounds. Spectacular monuments such as Mount Rushmore are also waiting along the way.

The 49th State: Alaska is a perennial RV destination. Noted for its unique scenic beauty, incredible vistas and abundant wildlife, Alaska is such a huge state, it's virtually impossible to take it all in on just a single trip. Clearly, fishing and sightseeing are the most common attractions. The scope of the trip is awesome, so do extensive planning and allow plenty of time to make it worthwhile. RV caravans to Alaska are popular, and may be worth considering for the first trip. However, going it alone allows time to linger along the way, find your own fishing places and take side trips on your own schedule.

Historic Sites and Museums: The oldest city in the U.S. is in Florida, the cradle of Liberty is in Massachusetts and the most-visited presidential library is in California. History comes alive at Williamsburg, Plymouth and in mining towns throughout the west. Indian traditions are celebrated in the Navajo Nation. We've been to a dinosaur museum in Colorado and the Spam museum, in Minnesota. Our wanderings allowed us to find lots of interesting, albeit little-known, museums and historic spots. Be curious when traveling…history, the arts and science are celebrated at many places throughout the land. You'll never know what gems you will find along the way.

Cities, Towns and Waterways: The largest city in the U.S. has over 8 million people. And, there are several towns in the U.S. where your visit can double the population. Traveling around in an RV allows you to explore America's diversity. Visit The Big Apple, the Luggage Capital of the World and the Crossroads of the West. Even though it's too congested to take your RV into big cities, don't avoid them. Stay in a campground on the outskirts, go into the city and take a guided tour to see the city and get an overview of its history and notable features. When traveling from sea to shining sea, give yourself the chance to wade in the Atlantic and Pacific oceans, Lake Michigan, the Gulf of Mexico and the Great Salt Lake…and to cross the Mighty Mississippi many times at multiple locations.

Where To Stay / Park It

Campgrounds and RV parks abound across the country. You see the familiar camping symbol on many interstate exits. In most parts of the country most of the year, campground and RV park sites are available on a drive-in/no reservation basis. However, common sense dictates that in very popular areas or heavily visited places (such as national parks during the summer) reservations are advisable. Snow birds also must plan ahead and make reservations well in advance if they want to ensure a spot for the warm winter season.

The most extensive campground listings can be found in the *North American RV Travel Guide*, which combines listings from the former *Trailer Life* and *Woodall's* directories. There are also a large number of directories and guides available that provide information about private campgrounds, RV parks, resorts, state and federal parks and locations for boondocking (free overnight parking).

The most comprehensive selection of campground guides can be found either at Camping World or in RV bookstores on the Internet. Browse at the bookstores, read the descriptions and ask other RVers which books they use for finding accommodations. There is no one single all-inclusive campground directory. You will eventually end up using the two, three or more books most suited to your style, preferences and needs. It's a trial and error process.

How Much Is "Too Much?"

Average daily campground fees can be as low as $25 or as high as $75 depending on your choices. Personal preferences and budget considerations will be key factors when you decide where to stay. Most directories and guides will spell out daily rates and provide at least a general description of the facility.

Savvy RV travelers quickly learn how to take advantage of the many discounts available to lower overall camping fees:

- Camping clubs can provide discounts from 10% to 50% off daily fees at selected campgrounds.

- Discount coupons can be found in directories and magazines and are distributed at RV shows and rallies.

- Some RVers find that boondocking every so often helps to offset escalating campground fees (see the next section in this chapter).

Once you begin traveling, you'll quickly learn about the types of RV parks and campgrounds out there as well as their fees. And you will be able to determine the kinds of campgrounds or RV parks and/or boondocking sites where you're most comfortable.

At some point, you may receive a solicitation from a campground membership organization offering a free stay at one of their RV parks or resorts in return for your attendance at a sales presentation. "Campground memberships" are different from "camping clubs." When RVers join a camping club, they are not required to sign a contract and the annual dues are usually small by comparison.

Campground memberships, on the other hand, can include a costly initial fee and requires a contract agreement to pay annual fees. While campground memberships may appear attractive during a sales presentation, it is important to gain sufficient RVing experience before making such a commitment. Some RVers find that campground memberships are suited to their travel schedules and the specific parks in the campground network are attractive enough to justify the investment. But some purchase only to find out later it was not suitable for them.

Boondocking

Boondocking is one of those topics that can cause a heated debate among RVers. Originally, boondocking was a way for campers to get as close as possible to nature by camping for free without hookups "out in the boonies." Lately, more urban boondockers can also be found taking advantage of the free overnight parking without hookups offered at some Walmarts, casinos and truck stops. They are referred to as "blacktop boondockers."

Out in the boonies, some free parking without hookups can still be found on Bureau of Land Management (BLM) federal land, Forest Service and some Army Corps of Engineers lands. Most of these areas are in western states, but some boondocking lands may be switched to fee-pay camping in the near future. When camping on federal lands, RVers should be responsible in caring for the land. Dispose of black and grey water tanks properly, limit the time you stay there and leave the area cleaner than you found it.

Blacktop boonies. The most popular locations for blacktop boondocking are Walmarts, casinos and truck stops. Always verify with security that overnight parking will be allowed before settling in for the night. Blacktop boondocking is useful for those occasions when you just want to pull in, get a full night's sleep and hit the road again the next morning. Be aware that blacktop boondocking is not camping. Don't put out the awning, chairs or barbeque – that's camping! If you want the outdoor comforts of camping, check into the nearest fee-pay campground. But when blacktop boondocking, restrict your activity to the interior of your rig. When you're in for a free overnight stay, you are there because of the hospitality of the property owner; be considerate. Don't litter and leave the area cleaner than you found it.

Blacktop Boondocking Etiquette

RVers should never abuse the hospitality of private businesses who allow free overnight parking. The Escapees RV Club established nine simple rules for proper overnight parking etiquette. Many other national RV clubs have adopted the creed as a model for their members as well. Be a considerate blacktop boondocker and observe these rules:

1) Stay one night only.

2) Obtain permission from a qualified individual.

3) Obey posted regulations.

4) No awning, chairs or barbecue grills.

5) Avoid using slideouts.

6) Do not use leveling jacks on asphalt.

7) Purchase gas, food or supplies as a form of thank-you when feasible.

8) Always leave an area cleaner than you found it.

9) Practice safety precautions.

Money-Saving Programs

Frequent visitors to public lands can get significant savings with the *America the Beautiful Senior Pass* or *Access Pass*. These are recreation passes issued by the federal government to provide a discounts on federal use fees for facilities and services such as camping, swimming, parking, boat launching and tours. It does not cover fees charged by concessionaires at federal facilities.

Senior Pass: This pass is for citizens of the United States who are 62 years of age or older. The cost for a senior pass is $10 and proof of age must be shown. It is a lifetime entrance pass to national parks, monuments, historic sites, recreation areas and national wildlife refuges that charge an entrance fee. The *Senior Pass* admits the pass signee and any accompanying passengers in a private vehicle.

Access Pass: This pass is for citizens of the United States who are blind or permanently disabled. The *Access Pass* is free; proof of medically-determined permanent disability must be shown. It is a lifetime entrance pass to national monuments, historic sites, recreation areas and national wildlife refuges that charge an entrance fee. The passport admits the pass signee and any accompanying passengers in a private vehicle.

Military: Active duty military and their dependents qualify for a free annual *America the Beautiful* pass.

Where To Obtain A Pass: The *Senior Pass* and *Access Pass* can be obtained in person at a federal recreation site, through an online application form, or through the mail. There is a $10 fee for passes ordered by mail. The annual *Military Pass* must be obtained in person. Federal recreation areas include the National Park Service, Bureau of Land Management, U.S. Forest Service, U.S. Fish & Wildlife Service and Bureau of Reclamation.

Online Resources

Blacktop Boondocking

www.overnightrvparking.com
Over 11,000 RV parking & no parking locations in U.S. and Canada. On Facebook & mobile devices, too.

www.travelbooksusa.com

Casino Camping: Lists hundreds of RV-Friendly casinos that permit free overnight parking or have RV Parks; state-by-state locator maps.

Walmart Atlas: Guide to over 4,000 Walmart stores, supercenters and Sam's Club stores in the U.S. Identifies availability of fuel.

Campgrounds & RV Parks

www.freecampsites.net
Community-driven platform for free camping locations.

www.campingroadtrip.com
18,000 campgrounds, RV parks & RV resorts on Camp Finder app (iPhone & Android). Free access to the list on website.

www.koa.com
Over 400 campgrounds. Free directory available. Locator maps online. Smartphone app available.

www.goodsamcamping.com
North American Travel Guide, combined listings from the former *Woodall's* and *Trailer Life* directories. Contains 13,500 listings. Digital version not available. Apps sold for smart phones.

www.freecampgrounds.com
Free and inexpensive (under $10) camping places listed by state.

www.gocampingamerica.com/search
Search for a campground or RV park in any state. Search by city, state or landmark name.

www.rvparkreviews.com
Reviews by campers of camping facilities throughout the U.S.

Camping on Public Lands

www.recreation.gov
Online reservations for camping at facilities managed by National Park Service, Forest Service, Army Corps of Engineers, Federal Bureau of Land Management, Bureau Of Reclamation and U.S. Fish and Wildlife Service.

www.travelbooksusa.com
Corps Camping and National Park Service guide books identify camping areas on federal land with roomy sites and hookups for big rigs.

www.nps.gov/findapark/passes.htm
Information on the *America the Beautiful* passes.

Clubs: Camping Membership

www.camphalfprice.com
Happy Camper Club has nearly 1,200 member campgrounds that offer half off camping fees. Find state locations online and in member directory. Low membership fee.

www.passportamerica.com
Passport America offers 50% discount; has over 1,800 member campgrounds. At website, click on state for campground locations. Low annual membership dues. Sponsors an annual rally.

www.coastresorts.com
Coast to Coast membership camping network of RV resorts and campgrounds; annual membership contract.

www.thousandtrails.com
Campground membership organization with 80 parks; purchase annual pass.

www.membershipresale.com
Specializing in resale of major campground membership contracts.

Education

www.rveducation101.com
RV training videos and DVDs.

Global Positioning Systems (GPS)

www.randmcnally.com
First company to develop RV-specific receiver, RVND GPS, 7-inch screen.

www.garmin.com
Garmin RV GPS, 7-inch screen.

www.magellen.com
Magellen RoadMate for RV GPS, 5-inch screen.

Online Travel Newsletters

www.rvtravel.com
Free weekly newsletter, daily RV tips covering RV and travel information.

www.wheellife.com
Timely information about RV lifestyle, people and destinations.

Trip Planning

www.campingroadtrip.com
Devoted to helping people plan road trips. Site includes a forum and campground listings.

www.googlemaps.com
Free online trip-planning tool. Pinpoints campground locations by state.

www.randmacnally.com
Publisher of the traditional Road Atlas.

www.travelbooksusa.com
Unique selection of travel and RV books.

www.rvbookstore.com
Books, CDs, magazines, videos, e-books and more.

Did you know...

RV camping clubs date back to the Tin Can Tourist of the 1920's and 1930's. Tin Can Tourist were groups of travelers who braved the dust and mud to drive their Lizzies (Model T's) across the U.S. before transcontinental roads were paved, camping by the side of the road, heating tin cans of food on a gasoline stove and bathing in cold water.

Chapter 10

All the Comforts of Home

"...Be it ever so humble, there's no place like home."
— *John Howard Payne*

Maintenance

Poll Question: What are your favorite hobbies in the RV?
Answer: The RV is my hobby.

While living out your retirement travel dream, you'll want to care for and protect the home that makes the dream possible.

My resident RV technician never tires of routine maintenance on the road. Indeed, the RV is his hobby; it's not only enjoyable, but he takes it very seriously! Here's a list of periodic maintenance activities you can place in the category of "must-dos"...unless you want to eventually see parts of your rig deteriorate before your very eyes. If you don't take the time to do the preventive and/or scheduled maintenance you'll eventually have to deal with emergency repair work.

Exterior Maintenance:

- Read all your manuals and follow maintenance guidelines.

- Water heater tanks should be flushed twice a year. Check the anode rod and replace when necessary.

- Have the propane lines and tank inspected by an authorized technician annually, and always turn off the propane at the tank before you roll. NEVER drive with the propane on.

- Change the water filter periodically.

- Check house and engine batteries every month for appropriate water levels.

- Clean exterior house compartments every couple of months. A good housecleaning ensures there are no stowaway bugs and bees down there.

- Check tire pressure every time you roll. Check lug nuts to be sure they're tight.

- Change oil and lubricate the engine every 3,000 to 5,000 miles.

- Change oil and filter on the generator periodically as recommended. Start and run the generator at least every two weeks with a full load capacity for at least 20 minutes.

- Keep the exterior of your vehicles clean. Wash 'em often!

- Wax your rig (or hire someone to do it) every six months.

- Clean and inspect the rubber roof quarterly. Look for any areas that may need to be re-sealed such as around vents, antennas and satellite. Use silicone spray on the TV antenna shaft to enable better sliding operation.

- Treat the slide seals with protective coating once a year or as needed (if drying out).

- Walk around and check the rig every time you stop.

- Use a proper size tire gauge to check inflation on all tires. Appropriate tire pressure varies so check on the side wall of each tire for the proper pressure.

Interior Maintenance:

- Complete routine interior housekeeping chores weekly…daily when in an area where sand, dirt or mud gets tracked in.

- Defrost refrigerator when interior fins get iced up.

- Clean and oil all wood surfaces every month or so to prevent drying.

- Stay organized by cleaning and straightening interior cabinets/drawers periodically. This will also prevent stowaway critters from moving in. You might find lost items such as sunglasses, TV remote, maps, even money.

- Check fire extinguisher gauges and smoke detector batteries periodically.

- Clean lint out of the clothes dryer after each use.

- Change filters on the heating/air system periodically.

Power & Plumbing

At a minimum every RVer needs to have a basic understanding of the three major on-board systems:

- Electrical
- LP Gas
- Plumbing

RV newbies will not completely learn about onboard systems all at once. Getting to know one's home on wheels is an ongoing process. RV owners find the process to be challenging and fun. The longer we reside in our RV, the more we learn about the onboard systems and how to utilize them most effectively and keep them in good working order.

Electrical Systems

Electricity is delivered to the RV in two ways: 12-volt DC (direct current) basic power is generated by the engine and coach batteries and regular 120-volt AC (alternating current) power comes from outside electric hookups or from an onboard generator.

Basic 12-volt electrical power for the RV comes from two battery sources – the engine (automotive) battery and the coach battery(ies). Both produce 12-volt DC power and both are kept charged by the vehicle engine (whether it's the engine in the motor home or the engine of the tow vehicle) and the alternator. The engine battery and the coach battery have different usage and storage capacities so the alternator is the device that keeps them appropriately charged.

The engine battery powers the engine of the motor home or tow vehicle plus its lights, horn, windshield wipers, radio, dashboard heater and air conditioner and electric brakes for a trailer. The battery(ies) in the coach provides 12-volt power to run interior lights, exhaust fans, water pump, alarm systems, LP and CO leak detectors, radio/stereo, power awning, hydraulic leveling systems and 12-volt appliances.

While the 12-volt system can support low voltage lights and exhaust fans, it simply does not have the muscle to provide the power needed for big-time appliances such as microwave and coffee pot. For regular electrical service – like what you get in a stick-built house – you need to tap into a 120-volt AC power source. You get this kind of service from an electric hookup at a campground or from an onboard generator.

The electrical equipment in an RV that needs 120-volt AC power in order to operate includes: coach heater and air conditioner, microwave, hair dryer, curling iron, coffee pot, toaster, computer and printer, VCR, TV, washer/dryer and refrigerator (although the refrigerator runs on more than one power source).

Campground and RV Park Hookups

The 120-volt hookups at campgrounds come in several strengths, depending on the amount of amperage they can deliver. Some older, antiquated campgrounds still have the very low 15 and 20-amp services. But, nowadays, 30-amp and 50-amp services are available at the majority of campgrounds and RV parks. The shape of the outlet indicates the amperage output. The older 15-amp and 20-amp outlets have just two prongs. A 30-amp outlet has two diagonal prongs at the bottom and a circular ground in the center above the prongs while a 50-amp outlet has three straight prongs at the bottom and a circular ground centered above the prongs. Most modern RVs need 30-amp or 50-amp to support their onboard equipment. Most new RVs come with a power cord suited to fit a 30-amp outlet; some deluxe RVs have a 50-amp cord. Whatever kind of power cord you have, be sure to get adapters to fit other amperage outlets and have them on hand in the RV.

What happens when you plug a 30-amp power cord (with an adapter) into a 20-amp outlet? Electrical connections will default to the lowest link. So in this case, you can expect to receive 20-amp service. Conversely, if you are rated for 30-amps and you plug in (with an adapter) to a 50-amp outlet, you'll only get 30-amps of power.

When you are plugged into a 120-volt power source, not only are you supporting the heavy-duty electrical appliances, but the 12-volt components are supported as well. A device called a converter, converts the AC power to DC in order to feed the 12-volt devices and eliminate drain on the engine and coach batteries.

When hooked up to electric power, it is wise to monitor the amperage usage as displayed on the control panel inside the RV. For example, if you are connected to 30-amp service, it means you can only use 30 amps at the same time. The control panel shows how many amps are currently being used. If you use several heavy-duty power-hungry appliances at once and exceed the amperage limitations, you are apt to trip a circuit breaker.

Generators

Another way to feed 120-volt power into the RV is from an onboard generator. A generator is standard equipment in most motorized RVs, but is less common in trailers. When camped away from hookups, the generator is the only way to power-up the larger equipment onboard. Most generators run on gas, although some run on diesel or propane. For the most part, generators in motorized RVs run off the same fuel source as the main motor. However, if they share the fuel with the motorized engine, the generator will automatically shut itself off when fuel levels drop to one-quarter of a tank, so it won't cause the vehicle to run out of gas or diesel fuel. It is always a good idea to plan ahead and have a full tank when you are planning to use the generator.

A gallon of gasoline or diesel fuel will usually keep a generator running for about two hours. A generator should be started and run for a minute or two before turning on 120-volt appliances. A generator can even be used while a motor home is en route. Cooling down a larger motor home on the go by using the dashboard air conditioner is practically impossible in very hot weather. So the generator can be employed to run the main air conditioner inside the coach.

What About Watts?

The power output of a generator is measured in watts. Know the output of your generator and guard against exceeding it. If you use too many 120-volt appliances and exceed the generator's capacity, you'll trip a circuit breaker (just like at home in the stick-built house). Most large onboard generators put out between 4,000 and 7,500 watts…some higher on big rigs. Small motor homes can have generators with a power output of 2,000 to 3,000 watts. When in doubt, check the owner's manual of your generator and of any major appliances to be able to monitor usage. Amp or watt draw is usually listed. To convert amps to watts and vice versa, use these formulas:

$$\text{Watts} \div \text{Volts} = \text{Amps}$$
$$\text{Amps} \times \text{Volts} = \text{Watts}$$

Generator Maintenance

Generators need to be run at least once a month in order keep them in shape; this process recirculates stagnant fuel and cleans the lines, the carburetor or fuel injectors. Other routine maintenance includes changing oil and filters and spark plugs. Be sure to read the generator operating manual for instructions about periodic maintenance.

Surge Protector

My resident electrician swears by his surge protector; it is a very important piece of equipment. When we are plugged in at an RV park, our rig and its electrical systems are at the mercy of power spikes or surges. The electrical pedestal outlet could short out or have faulty wiring. The electrical systems onboard our motor home can get fried by a power surge. A high-quality surge protector is well worth the money! I also keep a separate surge protector on the computer.

LP Systems

Another important power source for the RV is LP gas, or propane as it's commonly called. LP is liquefied petroleum. It is a gas. But propane is sold in liquid form and is stored in a container on the outside of the RV. Once it is released, the vapor trapped inside the tank works its way through the gas lines connected to appliances on board. It is a clean-burning and efficient fuel.

Propane is used primarily to fuel appliances associated with heat. It can power the gas range and oven and the RV furnace. It can also run the water heater, although in many

RVs the water heater can run off either electric or LP gas. The refrigerator is the other appliance that can run either on LP gas (propane) or electric.

Since the refrigerator is the one appliance onboard that must continuously be powered up, newer model refrigerators are manufactured so they can operate on one of three sources — 12-volt from battery, 120-volt from electrical hookup (or generator) or LP gas. A mode setting on the door of the fridge enables an RVer to switch among the settings. Typically, the refrigerator's power source is split, depending on whether the RV is moving or parked, plugged in to a power source or dry-camped. Modern RV refrigerators have an auto-select that automatically adjusts itself to the appropriate power source. When the RV is in motion, the 12-volt power source is recommended for the refrigerator. Do not use propane to power the fridge while traveling. Remember, the engine must be running for the 12-volt selection.

Hot water tanks are either six or 10-gallon. When the RV is plugged into campground electricity and is running several appliances, an RVer can use propane for operating the water heater, thus alleviating the amperage burden. For showers on the road when electric hookups aren't available, the hot water by propane is also handy. When using propane to heat water, most systems have a DSI (direct spark ignition) so you do not have to go outside to light the pilot with a match.

Most of the time, RVers are following the sun. But for the days (and nights) when it gets chilly, LP gas provides very nice forced-air heat throughout.

Cooking with gas is quite easy on board the RV. Most new cook top ranges even come equipped with igniters that create the spark to light the three or four stove-top gas burners. In the gas oven, all you need to do is locate the pilot light, turn on the gas, strike a match to light the pilot light and you're ready for some roasting or baking.

Unlike electrical power, LP gas (propane) has to be stored in a tank and carried with you. There are no propane "hookups" at campgrounds, although some campgrounds have an LP station where you can purchase propane to fill the tanks. Typically, propane is stored in one of two types of containers:

> DOT tanks (always white…don't ever paint them!) are usually mounted on the front of a trailer and can be removed and carried to get them

refilled. Smaller versions of the DOT tanks are sometimes used to power table-top gas grills.

ASME LP gas containers are mounted horizontally to the RV in an exterior storage compartment and can't be removed. Pull up to the LP gas station for a refill.

Removable propane tanks should always remain in the same mounted position. Never reinstall them in a different position as this can cause the liquid petroleum instead of the vapors to pour into the lines, creating a very dangerous situation. The same rule applies when refilling or during transport.

When you turn the propane tank valve to the open position, propane then flows through the lines of the coach to the appliances it will fuel. For safety sake, propane should be off while the RV is in transit.

Plumbing Systems

Fresh water and waste water systems are complex but they are surprisingly easy to use. Simply stated, your RV has a tank full of fresh water that provides hot and cold water for all the inside and outside faucets, for drinking, cooking, cleaning, showering, operating the washer and water for flushing the toilet. The RV has two other tanks: a grey water tank for holding waste water from the kitchen sink, shower and tub, washing machine and bathroom sink, and a black water tank for holding waste from the toilet. It is logical that the supply of fresh water must be replenished periodically and the grey water and black water tanks must be emptied (dumped) periodically. Thus summarizes the continuous cycle of the RV plumbing systems.

Fresh Water

An RV can have a continuous uninterrupted flow of fresh water by simply hooking up to a water outlet at a campground. The water comes into the RV through an inlet usually marked as "city-water hookup" and found on the driver's side of the RV. Always use a clean, white "drinking water" version of a hose; keep two 25-foot lengths of the clean hose in an RV storage compartment. Reserve these specially-designated hoses only for fresh water coming into the RV. Store them in a clean dry place; connect both ends together when storing to keep dirt and debris out of the hose. Storing the hoses in a clean plastic bag is helpful and be sure to replace the hose if it shows cracks. Do not use just any old garden hose; you wouldn't like the rubbery taste of the drinking water. We also use a filter between the fresh water source and the RV. In many parts of the country city drinking water needs to be filtered. Remember the surge protector recommended for an electrical connection? The water connection needs some added protection as well…a water pressure regulator will override any damaging force coming out of the water connection at a campground or RV park. Remember, delicate plastic piping on an RV is not the same as copper pipes in a stick-built house.

When you're on the road or out in the boonies, the full fresh water tank provides an ample supply of fresh water for a few days or more, depending on your usage. Know how much fresh water your tank holds and continue to monitor its level on the control panel inside the RV. When it's time to refill the fresh water tank, replenish fresh water at a campground, RV park, rest stop, truck stop or any place that offers fresh drinking water. Most RVs have a simple gravity fill valve for the clearly designated fresh water tank fill. Once again, use your fresh water hose and a filter. A 12-volt water pump dispenses needed water throughout the RV when it's not connected at a campground.

The Toilet

Just about every type of RV is outfitted with a marine-style toilet. Water levels and flushing are controlled by floor pedals. Once the toilet is flushed, clean water can be put back into the toilet by stepping on one of the foot pedals. There should be enough water left in the toilet to keep the seals from drying out but not too much that it would spill out in transit. Use only toilet paper recommended for marine/RV toilets and use only sanitizer and chemicals designed to break down waste that are specifically designed for RV toilets. The cleaning agents you may have used in the stick-built house could be harmful to plastic appliances and hoses.

Dumping the Tanks

If done carefully and properly, the task of dumping the tanks will not be a problem. When the black water and grey water tank levels indicate it's time to dump, find a dump station. Be sure to wear rubber gloves during the dumping procedure. Connect one end of your sewer hose to the single sewer outlet below the black and grey flush valves and place the other end into the in-ground sewer opening at the dump station. Be sure to stick the hose well into the in-ground sewer opening to prevent it from slipping out when you start emptying the tank. It is important to be sure the hose is secure at both ends before you open either valve. Next, test your setup by opening the grey water valve for about 30 seconds to let a small amount of grey water run through to be sure there are no tears or leaks in the sewer hose and to verify that the sewer end of the hose is in the ground securely. Note: this is just a test; the full grey water tank will be dumped last (following the black water tank dumping). But this additional small task will help you avoid any black water spills and embarrassment. Sewer hoses can develop tears and splits from continued use…and you want to avoid black water spills at all costs!

Always empty the black water tank first. When you pull the valve open, the black water tank empties. Next, close the black water valve and pull the grey water release valve. Dumping the tanks in this order allows the grey water to flush out any accumulated black water waste that may be caught in the hose. Even though there are two valves, both tanks empty through the same hose. After the grey water tank empties, close the valve. Remove the connection from the RV first; hold the hose up high as you walk back to the sewer connection so excess water will drain from the hose into the sewer. Wash your sewer hose and store it in a separate compartment, preferably in its own heavy plastic bag. Do not store sewer hoses near the fresh water hose. Use the water hose provided at the dump — or your own green flushing hose (sometimes the hose at the dump station "disappears") — to clean up the ground around the sewer connection.

Always use the exact same procedure for dumping the tanks and be meticulous about wearing gloves, avoiding spills and leaving the area clean. Tanks can be dumped either at a dump station or at a campsite that has a sewer connection. After you've washed your hands, place the appropriate amount of approved toilet chemical into the black water tank, along with several flushes of fresh water. It is always a good idea to have some water sloshing around in the black water tank while you're on the road. It helps to keep the inside wall of the tank reasonably clean.

Clean Black Water Tank

Most newer motor homes and trailers have a separate "flush" inlet into the black water tank; the inlet is clearly identified. This allows you to periodically force fresh water into the tank for cleaning/flushing. Flushing should be done after about every third or fourth dumping. Be sure you are using the green hose for this purpose. In older model RVs, the best way to handle this task is to use a water wand attached to the end of a green cleaning hose to force water into the tank via the toilet. Also, use approved chemicals for the black water tank to protect the tank and eliminate odors. Be sure to follow directions on the product package.

It goes without saying that RVers must be good stewards of the environment. Always use proper dumping procedures, be careful and always clean up any inadvertent spills.

Tools

What kinds of tools should you carry along in order to get all your maintenance tasks (and more) done? When we decided to go on the road full time, my husband had scores of tools stashed in our two-car garage and even more stored in a shed. When D-Day (decision day) arrived and he had to pick which tools would come with us, I came to learn that guys have a sentimental attachment to their tools. Holding a well-worn pair of pliers, he exclaimed, "Do you realize I've had these since I was an apprentice. They sure don't make 'em like this any more." I had to keep reminding him that the storage bins in the motor home won't have the same capacity as the garage and shed.

Nevertheless, there are essential tools that no self-respecting RVer should be without. The checklists below enumerate the items that should be in your tool box and storage bins.

Tool Box:

> Claw hammer
> Screwdriver (flat head and Phillips)
> Pipe wrench
> Crescent wrench
> Socket wrench and sockets
> Pliers – regular and needle nose
> Box cutter and X-Acto knife
> Ammeter
> Propane lighter
> Plumbers tape
> Hose and sink washers
> Assorted fuses

Assorted nails and screws

Bungee cords of various sizes

Electric drill

Duct tape

Gas siphon

Funnel

Flashing light for road emergencies

Supplies For The Vehicle:

Windshield washer fluid

Brake fluid

Transmission fluid

Oil

WD-40

Cleaning supplies

Essential External RV Stuff:

Sewer hoses and couplers

Collapsible support for sewer hose

Sewer elbow adapter for drain

Sewer adapter for RV

Spare valve cap

Two hose clamps

25-foot electrical extension cable

15, 20 & 30 amp adapters

Two 25-foot water hoses

15-foot satellite cable

A hands-free light

Tire knocker

Gloves

Pulling In and Out of Campgrounds

Setting up and breaking camp routines are second nature for experienced RVers. But for the newbie these tasks can be overwhelming. Even though the dealer or seller did a walk-through and showed you how to hook up your RV, the first few times will be trial and error. We've all been there. In the beginning, it's a good idea to pull into a campground to set up by mid-afternoon. This will ensure that other campers will be around to give you a hand, should you need it.

When backing into the campsite, someone (generally the co-pilot) should guide the driver while backing into the space. It's the guide's job to get the RV into the middle of the site, to be sure you don't back into a tree and to watch for low hanging branches. After your vehicle is in, do a walk-around to be sure there's enough room for slideouts. Check the electric box, water connection and sewer hookup.

- ✓ Put the jacks down and slides out.
- ✓ Plug in electric. Use the appropriate adapter for the connection and always use a surge protector.
- ✓ Attach water hose.
- ✓ Attach sewer hose.
- ✓ Attach cable TV (if applicable)

Getting the rig ready to go back on the road requires both inside and outside preparations. With two people traveling together, responsibilities could be divided with the driver handling outside and the co-pilot taking care of the inside.

Outside:

- ✓ Dump black and grey water tanks.
- ✓ Fill fresh water tank. Always use a filter before taking on unfamiliar fresh water.
- ✓ Disconnect and store water hose.
- ✓ Disconnect and store sewer hoses.
- ✓ Turn off propane. Never travel with propane on.
- ✓ Disconnect power cord. Disconnect cable TV.
- ✓ Bring down TV antenna or satellite dish.
- ✓ Bring in awnings and secure. Stow outside furniture and grill.
- ✓ Secure outside cabinet doors.
- ✓ Check & latch the roof pod (if applicable).
- ✓ Do a visual check of the tires.
- ✓ Bring in slides. Retract jacks. Be sure all obstacles are cleared before

retracting slideout rooms.

✓ Retract steps on travel trailers.

✓ Do a general walk around check of the campsite.

✓ Hook up the tow vehicle or toad.

✓ Check the hitch and be sure the tow bar is secure. Check that transmission on the toad is in neutral. Always do a pull test before pulling out completely.

✓ Check brake lights, turn signals, foot brake and tow brake.

Inside:

✓ Secure all doors, cabinets and drawers; stow coffee pot.

✓ Clear kitchen, bathroom & bedroom counters.

✓ Remove all obstacles to slide rooms to be retracted.

✓ After tanks are dumped, put sanitizer in toilet and close lid.

✓ Check refrigerator setting.

✓ Check that propane oven and stove are off.

✓ Secure pet dishes.

✓ Close windows and vents.

✓ Secure laptop computer. Check that cell phones are in place.

✓ Record mileage in log book.

✓ Do a general walk around to be sure all loose items in all rooms are secured.

Create Your Own Checklists

Every RV is a little different, so it's a good idea to make up your own personal checklists, tailored for your rig, whether it's a motor home with a dinghy or fifth wheel with a tow truck. Have two lists — one for arrival and one for departure. Use information from the preceding sections, or use the *Checklist Resources* at the end of this chapter as models. This is an important exercise and it can help you to avoid such costly errors as forgetting to lower the antenna or pulling out of the site with the electric still plugged in, or not retracting the steps on the fifth wheel.

Be sure to have a checklist for arrival and departure. If traveling as a couple, share the responsibilities and double-check one another. You can never be too meticulous where your safety and equipment are concerned.

The Top Five

Safety checks and meticulous attention to routine maintenance can keep you safe and happy on the road. The top five RV insurance claims—as reported by GMAC—may help you to understand just how important maintenance is.

Claim #1: Refrigerator fires and propane tanks. GMAC Insurance receives at least 400 claims per year due to refrigerator fires caused by leaking propane tanks. A rig can burn up in as few as six minutes as a result of propane leaks. Also, propane tanks can overheat when the outside of the tank has been painted. Sports fans have been known to paint their tanks with team colors, but dark colors absorb the sun's rays faster and this can cause the tank to overheat and explode.

Safety Tip #1: Have propane tank lines and connections checked annually by a certified dealer and don't paint the outside of the propane tank.

Claim #2: Hitting gas station overhangs and bridges.

Safety Tip #2: Always remember your RV's height. If your memory is not too sharp, tape a note to your dashboard.

Claim #3: Forgetting to retract steps and awnings. These attachments can get torn off if they're sticking out and that leaves a nasty hole in your rig.

Safety Tip #3: Follow the pre-flight checklist.

Claim #4: Tire blowouts. Two major causes of blowouts are over or under inflated tires and worn out tires.

Safety Tip #4: Clean your tires; keep them blocked from the sun when parked. Check tire pressure regularly. Have wheel alignment checked periodically. Replace worn tires.

Claim #5: Animal infestation. RVs sitting unused during off season, especially in winter, can attract mice and squirrels looking for a cozy home. These critters chew wires and lines, not to mention the mess they can make.

Safety Tip #5: Start the RV once a week to scare them away.

Why No Spare?

There was a time when recreational vehicles came equipped with a spare tire. Not so anymore. With larger, heavier vehicles coming on the road, it becomes very risky – if not downright impossible – for anyone but a trained technician with proper equipment to change a flat. Consequently, including a spare tire became a liability issue for manufacturers. Spare tires are available as after-market products. But we'd suggest purchasing a road service contract instead. If you get a flat, leave the tire changing to the professionals.

Recalls

Nowadays vehicle manufacturer recalls are a fact of life. Recalls can occur for RV's, trucks and toads that were made anywhere from last year to several years ago. When a recall takes place it can apply to virtually millions of vehicles. You wouldn't want to miss it if your vehicle happens to be among them. The National Highway Safety Administration maintains a database of recalls at www.recalls.gov. You can also find recalls reported in major RV magazines.

Online Resources

Checklists

www.rv-roadtrips.thefuntimesguide.com/checklists/
Good advice plus links to effective checklists to use as models.

www.changingears.com/rv-sec-checklists/
Printable arrival and setup checklists for trailers and motor homes.

Android and iPhone apps
RV Checklist app; free for Android; $.99 for iPhone

Dump Stations

www.rvdumps.com
Find RV dump stations throughout the country.

www.sanidumps.com
Lists dump stations in the U.S. and Canada.

Maintenance

www.rvdoctor.com
View articles about RV maintenance & safety, post a technical question or read previous questions and answers.

www.rveducation101.com
Comprehensive site with information about using and maintaining your recreational vehicle.

www.doityourselfrv.com
Click on *Projects* tab for articles on maintenance and repairs.

RV Recall Information

www.recalls.gov
National Highway Traffic Safety Administration (NHTSA) database of all vehicle recalls (including recreational vehicles) listed by make, model and year.

Supplies

www.campingworld.com
Supplies, equipment, RV accessories, service, etc.

www.rvupgrades.com
Specializes in unique RV accessories and supplies.

www.walmart.com/cp/RV-accessories/1070265
RV accessories and supplies. Free store pickup.

Chapter 11

The RV Community on the Road

"Come my friends, 'tis not too late
To seek a newer world."
— *Alfred Lord Tennyson*

An overriding characteristic of RVers is their strong sense of community. This fact may seem incongruous when describing people who are travelers in solitary rigs, separated most of the time by the many road miles between them…not to mention their diverse backgrounds or dissimilar occupations and income levels. But RVers are a tight-knit community of like-minded people who consider one another friends. When a couple of RVers meet for the first time – it's amazing – they are instant buddies.

The first time I saw this phenomenon play out was at an interstate rest area during our first trip across the state of Kansas. My husband was walking around our rig, checking the tires, the toad and doing whatever else the pilot does before taking off. I looked out the window and saw him on the other side of the parking lot with some strange guy. Together they were examining the guy's rig, chatting, laughing and acting like a couple of long-lost brothers. They shook hands enthusiastically and slapped each other on the back when they parted company. I know my husband doesn't have a brother, so I assumed he happened to meet an old friend or relative by chance. "Who was that guy," I asked later, "Someone you know from work?"

"No, of course not. He's just a guy…an RVer!" he said, not realizing I didn't understand that special bond, the unique connection among people sharing the RV lifestyle. The bond is especially evident with full-time or near full-time RVers. Since that long-ago incident in Kansas I've had the privilege of being assimilated and accepted into the village with no boundaries, that special place on the road known as "The RV Community." On the road, living, traveling in an RV we are never alone, nor are we ever disconnected from a supportive network no matter how far out in the woods we happen to be.

Campgrounds and RV parks are particularly friendly. People living in permanent neighborhoods often experience situations where they hardly ever interact with neighbors, even live across the street from people they've never met. But that doesn't happen in the RV community. RV parks, resorts and campgrounds are the friendliest neighborhoods on the road! Whether people are in for a single night or a couple of weeks, in-season or off-season, camaraderie prevails. Impromptu social gatherings as well as scheduled activities are common at campgrounds and RVers are welcome to get as involved as they want. But folks in the RV community are not pushy. If you're not a "joiner" your privacy is respected.

RV Clubs and Rallies

RVers are quite sociable and enjoy being together. So it's only natural that they would form clubs and camp together. Clubs provide organized activity, opportunities to travel together and many other benefits. The oldest camping club was founded in 1966 by a group of RVers who wanted to put "Good Samaritan" bumper stickers on their rigs so fellow members would know where they could get help on the road. The founding "Good Sams" firmly established a spirit of helpfulness that is traditional among RVers to this day.

Scores of camping clubs are currently going strong. The largest are nationwide organizations comprised of a network of local chapters where most of the activity takes place. Local chapters camp together once or twice a month at different campgrounds with specific activities scheduled plus lots of free time for fun and fellowship. The proverbial "pot luck supper" is a staple of club camp-outs. Members join in card games and dominos at the campground's activity hall most evenings. Once or twice a year local chapters throughout a state or region come together for a larger camping event called a rally. The agenda for rallies can include games, special events, seminars, entertainment and, oh yes, still more food, fun and fellowship. Gathering around the evening campfire is a traditional way to end the day. Once a year, local chapters from all the states and regions travel to a national rally, which is a still larger and more elaborate version of the state and regional events.

The three major RV/camping clubs are: Good Sam, FMCA, and Escapees.

Good Sam Club

Good Sam, the largest camping club, is open to all types of RVs, trailers and camping units. It has more than 1.5 million members. Its stated goal is to make RVing safer and more enjoyable and save members money through club-endorsed benefits and services. The now familiar decal of the smiling face crowned by the Good Samaritan halo can be seen on many rigs throughout the U.S.

Annual dues are minimal and most members reap rewards over and above the annual cost of membership through the ten percent campground discount program. Members also receive the popular monthly magazine *Highways* that contains general RV and travel information as well as news from club chapters around the country. The popular magazine is available in print and digital versions.

Good Sam's many members are organized into local chapters that hold camping get-togethers throughout the year. Chapters within a state get together for Samborees, state-wide rallies that include fellowship, entertainment and seminars. Samboree schedules are listed in *Highways* magazine and traveling Good Sam members often attend rallies in other states.

Good Sam, Camping World and several other affiliated companies sponsor national rallies that attract thousands of participants. These events feature seminars, entertainment, games, events, outings, vendors and manufacturers' displays of the newest models of various kinds of RVs.

Benefits to Good Sam members include free trip routing service, ten percent discount at hundreds of campgrounds and RV parks in the U.S. and Canada and discounts at Camping World. Good Sam sells its own Emergency Road Service plan. It also offers discounted rates on RV and car insurance and extended warranties. The club has its own credit card service.

The Good Sam organization also provides a venue for members to buy and sell RVs, obtain financing, purchase parts, supplies and service for the RV and make campground reservations.

FMCA

Family Motor Coach Association was founded in 1963 by a group of people who owned what at the time they called "house cars." It has grown into an international organization for families who own and enjoy the recreational use of motor homes. Membership is open to motor homes only, not trailers or any other type of RV. As the FMCA gained popularity, members decided that the best way to enjoy fellowship on a regular basis was to form into sub-groups or chapters. Now there are about 500 chapters in 10 regions and FMCA has a centralized national governing board to coordinate club activities.

FMCA's local chapters hold casual campground rallies throughout the year, usually on weekends and at locations not far from members' homes. This gives them a chance to use their motor homes more often without traveling great distances. Area rallies, larger than the chapter events, include exhibits, seminars and entertainment as well as the traditional fun, food and fellowship.

The annual FMCA International Convention is popular and well-attended. Thousands of motor coaches congregate for themed events featuring fellowship, games, outings, headline entertainment, educational seminars and workshops. RV manufacturers display the latest models of motor homes and hundreds of vendors display a wide variety of goods and services of interest to RVers.

Since its inception FMCA has issued more that 350,000 memberships. Currently, there are over 80,000 RVing families active in FMCA activities. The popular FMCA magazine is published monthly.

The Escapees (SKP) Club

Founded in 1978 to provide a support network for RVers, members of the Escapee club are referred to by the acronym SKPs. The organization started with fewer than 100 families and, since its inception, has grown to over 60,000. The familiar club logo – seen affixed to the back of many an RV on the road – is a house in a wagon. The Escapee support network is based on the concept of sharing and caring. By comparison to other clubs, it is less commercialized.

The mission of Escapees is to provide support for RV families by meeting the basic needs of friendship and camaraderie among people who share a similar lifestyle. The parking aspect of Escapees is one thing that differentiates this club from the rest. Escapees own and operate a system of parks. Low-cost, short term parking is available at their parks for members who just want a safe place to stop for a few days as well as economical rates for those who want full service camping for longer terms. There are also lots available for lease at some parks for those who want to establish a home base there or need long-term accommodations.

SKP's sponsor an annual rally, called Escapade, at a different location each year. They also publish a monthly magazine, have local chapters and operate an extensive website that includes a high-participation, popular RV Forum. Escapees also conduct political action to preserve RVers' rights. SKPs operate a day-care center, called CARE, at their home base in Texas for ailing members.

Special interest groups within the Escapees club include: Disaster Operations Volunteers, who mobilize to assist the American Red Cross when needed, and Habitat For Humanity. The SKP Elks Group is also involved in charity works, scholarships and continuing support for the CARE Center.

Escapees is incorporated in the state of Texas and has its headquarters there. It offers a mail-forwarding service used by many full-timers because of its efficiency.

Although originally founded for full-time RVers, SKP is now open to all RVers who continue to be attracted to the club's persistent and enduring philosophy of caring about people.

Special Interest Clubs

Fellowship is the bedrock of the RV Community. Many people belong to more than one club. For instance, an RVer may join one of the three major organizations for the discounts or benefits, but look to other clubs for socializing and regular camping activities.

To name but a few, there's: SMART (Special Military Active Retired Travel Club), NAARVA (National African American RVers Association), NCT (National Masonic Camping Travelers), FCRV (Family Campers & RVers), Christian Campers, FlyFishers, Quilters, Bikers, Under 55, Over 55, Singles, Women, Loners, etc. The Explorer RV Club is Canada's largest.

For RVers interested in volunteer work, there's Volunteers on Wheels, a Christian organization that responds to places and/or occurrences where volunteers are needed. The Escapees Club has an active Habitat for Humanity group.

Major camping organizations have also formed sub sets called special interest groups or BOFs (Birds of a Feather), namely: Barbershop Harmony, Computer Users, Coaches for Christ, Frustrated Maestros, Rolling Red Hats, Square Dancing, Woodcarvers, etc.

RV Manufacturers Brand Owner Clubs

Just about every RV manufacturer sponsors a "brand club" and many hold rallies and get-togethers all year. When you purchase an RV, new or used, it behooves you join the manufacturer's owners' club…dues are usually modest and the benefits are many. One of the largest manufacturer clubs is Winnebago-Itasca Travelers (WIT). Their annual "Grand National Rally," held in July, all but doubles the population of the little town of Forest City, Iowa, home of Winnebago Industries and birthplace of the thousands of coaches in attendance.

RV club choices are many. The Good Sam website offers up a list of more than 100 clubs for RVers to consider, FMCA lists their special interest groups and Escapees lists their BOF's (Birds of A Feather) groups in their magazines.

Online RV Communities and Forums

The World Wide Web is a favorite place for RVers to get together in large RV communities. RVers are always willing, ready and able to provide help, advice and (yes) opinions on all topics related to RVing and some that aren't. So it's no surprise that RVers should come together on a forum, where someone starts a discussion and everyone who reads it chimes in with a comment. The oldest RV-related online community, formed about 20 years ago, is RVForum.net. Its members participate in a number of mini rallies, many are spontaneous, all promote fellowship. The three major RV Clubs also have forums on their respective websites. The rvnetwork.com, sponsored by Escapees, has a wealth of full-time RVers among those who share information on a regular basis.

iRV2.com is a leading online forum community for RV owners that offers diverse forums. The purpose of iRV2 is to foster a friendly atmosphere for members to exchange knowledge about their motor homes and trailers and their travels. It also features campground reviews and information about buying, selling and repairing RVs. iRV2 also sponsors a large annual rally.

If you are looking for information or just want a place to chat with like-minded individuals about RV-related issues, join a forum or two. Membership is free. Most of the sites have advertising, but the main focus is discussion, news and opinions. When it comes to the advice on the forums (and there's plenty of it), most forum members will agree with the premise: don't rely on just one source for information on RVing.

RV Caravans

A popular activity is the RV caravan. Various companies, some affiliated with major RV clubs and organizations, offer these planned group excursions to destinations such as Mexico in winter and Alaska in summer. The tour company organizes a trip for a group of RVs that has a planned itinerary, with reservations made for campground accommodations each night and arrangements for tour stops and activities along the way. A wagonmaster RV leads the caravan and a tailgunner RV brings up the rear to ensure everyone in the caravan arrives safely. The tailgunner is also responsible to help anyone who may experience mechanical problems along the way.

RV caravans can be a long-weekend away or a two or three-week excursion. The Copper Canyon/Piggyback tour is a popular one, where caravanning RVs get to spend part of the trip hitched to flat railroad cars as traveling attendees see Mexico's famed Copper Canyon from the train. Other guided tours are offered to various well-known spots. For example, RVers can purchase a tour through Canada, a trip to the Rose Bowl Parade at year-end, a tour to see the cherry blossoms in spring to Washington, DC, or the perennially-popular caravan to Alaska.

Online Resources

Caravans & Tours

www.fantasyrvtours.com
Guided RV vacations around the world.

www.rvalaskatours.com
RV tours to Alaska.

www.adventurecaravans.com
Guided tours in the United States, Canada, and Mexico.

www.yankeervtours.com
Unique escorted package tours in the U.S. and Canada.

Clubs & Online Forum Communities

www.goodsamclub.com
Good Sam Club, the nation's largest camping club.

www.rv.net
Open Roads Forum, largest on the web. Affiliated with Good Sam, Trailer Life, Woodalls and Motor Home.

www.fmca.com
Family Motor Coach Association for motor home owners. Has many manufacturer-specific clubs. Active forum.

www.escapees.com
Club founded as a support and service network for RVers. Sponsors a good Boot Camp for newbies.

www.rvnetwork.com
Forum sponsored by Escapees, high participation by experienced, knowledgeable RVers.

www.iRV2.com
Leading online forum community; diverse forums. Sponsors and promotes rallies.

www.RVForum.net

The oldest RV-related online community. Mini rallies. Forum popular with retirees.

www.RV-Dreams.com/forum

Friendly forum to collect and share information. Sponsors and promotes rallies.

Clubs: Special Interest

www.rvingwomen.com

National network with chapters throughout the U.S. Sponsors rallies and educational events.

www.lonersonwheels.com

Club for single campers and travelers; not a matchmaking or dating service.

www.naarva.com

National African-American RVers Association.

www.gonct.org

National Camping Travelers, a Masonic family camping club.

www.explorer-rvclub.com

Canada's largest RV club.

www.fcrv.org

Family campers and RVers, dedicated to camping fellowship. Local chapters, monthly campouts, annual Campvention.

Chapter 12

Supplement Your Income

"…the privilege to work is a gift, the power
to work is a blessing, the love of work is success."
— *David O. McKay*

Working on the Road

Today larger numbers of retirees are working well into their 60's and 70's. This trend is expected to continue. Retirement isn't what it used to be. People who opt for RVing during their retirement years will find many job opportunities out there. Typically, retirees who work while RVing are doing so to supplement their income. Consequently, their jobs on the road are part-time or contract opportunities that rarely include health insurance benefits. For the most part, retirees look for jobs that will provide what's commonly referred to as "walking around money." The choice comes down to what do you want to do and how much do you want or need to make.

There are also many (mostly younger) people living and working on the road who are not retired. These folks need to be employed in positions that will pay enough to be their primary source of income. More often than not they seek full time jobs with benefits. However, since this book is written specifically for retirees and near-retirees, the employment opportunities discussed here focus on the positions usually filled by retired persons.

Employment opportunities for RVing retirees generally fall into three broad categories:

1) Jobs where you stay in one location for specific lengths of time,

2) Jobs where you move from place to place in order to work,

3) Jobs that can be done anywhere, while on the move or in a single location.

Seasonal Work

Among the major job sources for RV retirees are campgrounds, RV parks and RV resorts. They can be either federal/state/county-operated or privately-owned facilities. They all need to hire temporary or seasonal workers to supplement their permanent year-round staff. Work camping is one of the fastest growing trends in the job market in the U.S.

The most popular position is that of campground host at a federal, state or county park. Camper host jobs generally require a total of 20 hours work per week in return for a free campsite for whatever period of time is agreed upon…a month or two or a season. The hours are filled by a single individual or by a couple. Among the tasks that may be required of the campground host(s) are greeting campers, registrations, assisting with finding and parking on the site, raking and cleaning camp sites and cleaning showers and rest rooms. These jobs are referred to as "volunteer" positions when there is no monetary salary included with the contract. Retirees are attracted to campground host jobs because it gives them an opportunity to stay free for extended periods of time in some of the country's most scenic places, with plenty of leisure time to relax and enjoy the outdoor activities. Privately-owned campgrounds and resorts also have host positions. They give the free campsite for 20 hours work per week and, further, pay an hourly salary for additional hours worked.

Other part time and full time positions available at campgrounds and RV resorts include: activities director, fishing guides, tour guides, registration and gift shop clerks, maintenance workers, management positions, security, food services, shuttle bus drivers, gatekeepers, food service staff and others.

The advantage of working in campgrounds is that there are campgrounds and RV parks all over the country. Thus RVers have their choice of locale and can vary their work locations season by season. Many employers – campgrounds and RV resorts – prefer to hire people who bring their own housing with them. Older workers are more dependable and when they live so close to the job, they're rarely late for work! When you apply for a position as campground host, don't be surprised if the employer asks for a photo of you and your rig with the application. Upscale resorts in particular want only clean and well-maintained (not necessarily brand new) rigs on their property. The condition of your rig says something about you…it tips off a prospective employer about your work habits.

Part time and full time seasonal jobs can be found at church camps, scout camps and camps for families of active and retired military. There are positions at amusement and theme parks, camping stores and seasonal resorts throughout the country.

Compensation varies broadly. Even when you secure a position that pays an hourly wage or weekly salary, a free site is usually part of the package. Some RVers manage to negotiate good compensation through a combination of wages and perks such as free site, free propane, free use of the laundry or tickets to local attractions. There are so many positions available, job seekers can be selective.

Snow birds who spend five or six months in a single sunny location can find seasonal jobs at many local establishments whose businesses increase during the season. Snow birds take jobs at retail stores, golf courses, restaurants, recreational facilities, tourist attractions and other places where the length of the employment contract exactly matches their time in the sunny locale.

Workers Moving Around

The classic job for those who like to travel around is RV delivery. Manufacturers hire drivers to deliver RVs from the factory to the dealer and dealers frequently hire drivers to take rigs to and from shows and rallies. Other popular jobs for RVers include the wagonmaster, tailgunner and technical positions in RV caravans.

Enterprising vendors carve out an income selling products that are of interest and value to RVers at local, state and national rallies and conventions sponsored by RV Clubs. Many vendors also follow the RVIA show circuit offering their products to the thousands of people who attend the shows sponsored by RV manufacturers. Others, particularly artisans, artists and crafters, sell their wares at flea markets, fairs and (the granddaddy of 'em all) the annual "swap meet" during the winter season in Quartzsite, AZ.

Other RVing jobs that require individuals to travel around include sales for campground advertising, campground inspectors and representatives for corporations that do business with RV parks, RVers and the RV industry. Musicians, stand-up comedians and other performers are in demand for gigs at RV club rallies. Some traveling preachers and musicians can go from church to church and get to see the country during the week.

Jobs Anywhere You Are

Resourceful RV retirees can always devise ways to make some extra income doing what they've done all their lives. Hair stylists, barbers, RV technicians, auto mechanics, massage therapists and tailors can all provide their professional services on an as-needed basis wherever they happen to be. Other services that can be marketed around the campground (with authorization from management) include RV washing, waxing and detailing and maintenance work. Entrepreneurial RV retirees often identify a need and develop products or services on the road that keep them challenged and make some extra money as well.

Some travelers who do not want to be tied down for a seasonal commitment will ask when they check into a campground if they need temporary help. This is an especially effective approach for people who have handyman or clerical skills and for tradesmen with specific skills such as electrician, carpenter, computers, etc. RVers have been known to pick up "walking around money" this way…obtaining temporary work spontaneously. We know of a person who does very well as a windshield chip repair person. All it took was a sign on the motor home advertising his skills at repairing windshield chips and his customers come to him.

The computer aboard most RVs opens an array of jobs that can be done anywhere. These include consulting, technical writing, creative writing and illustrating, investments, business consulting and special projects, to name a few.

How to Find the Jobs

Employment positions discussed in this chapter are just a small portion of the jobs being filled by RV retirees. They are examples of the thousands of jobs that become available continuously nationwide. How do you learn about them?

The Internet is the primary source. Employment ads also appear in the classified sections of RV magazines. Snow birds can use their local newspaper's employment classifieds as a source in their seasonal location.

The Workamper website is the largest employment service for RV travelers. It charges an annual membership fee and matches RVers with employers and visa versa. Founded in 1987, its publication, *Workamper News* is available in print and online. They also offer daily hotline job notifications and resume service. Workamper sponsors job fairs that attract RVers who want to work and employers who want to hire them.

A leading employer of campers is *Recreation Resource Management*, a private company that operates campgrounds and other recreational facilities in national forests and state parks. It manages some 175 sites in 11 states. The company maintains a work camping website –www.camphost.org – where persons seeking campground host positions may obtain information and complete an online application.

Online Resources

Work Opportunities

www.workamper.com
Brings job seekers and employers together.

www.work-camping.com
Work camping jobs at Recreation Resource Management areas.

www.camphost.org
Information about becoming a campground host at Recreation Resource Management areas.

www.nps.gov/personnel
This site is designed to provide basic information on career opportunities with the National Park Service.

www.fs.fed.us/fsjobs
Temporary employment opportunities with the U.S. Forest Service.

www.yellowstonejobs.com
Yellowstone National Park employment site.

www.nps.gov/yose/jobs/
Yosemite National Park employment options.

www.workatkoa.com
Job opportunities at KOA Campgrounds.

www.workersonwheels.com
Jobs and resources for full-timers, work campers, and other RVers.

Epilogue

"These are a few of my favorite things…"
— *from The Sound of Music*

As full-time travelers who crisscrossed the country many times, we often hear:

QUESTIONS:

  1) Don't you ever get tired of traveling?

  2) Have you been to every state?

  3) What's your favorite place?

  4) What state is the nicest?

  5) I have limited vacation time, what place would you suggest?

ANSWERS:

  1) No, we never tire of traveling.

  2) Every state but Hawaii (for obvious reasons).

  3) We have too many "favorite" places to single out a #1.

  4) Wherever we happen to be. Every state has its own unique charm.

  5) Depends on your interests, likes (and dislikes).

In our travels, sometimes we're typical tourists and other times explorers on the back roads. Listed below are a few of our favorites…places, people and experiences. These items appear in no particular order since a ranking is impossible.

  ❋ Mt. Rushmore and the Black Hills area. An ultimate tourist adventure and our initial exposure to the knowledgeable National Park Service Rangers.

  ❋ The Redwood Forest. What an awesome experience driving the big rig through a forest full of the big trees. Photos don't capture the mammoth beauty.

* Little "coffee huts" all over the state of Washington, where the latte is always good and served with a straw sticking out of the hole in the top of the cup (not usually seen in the East).

* Stately Saguaros in Arizona. The gentle giants of the desert fill the hillsides. They're a sight to behold as they stand silently trying to guard the desert's fragile ecosystem.

* Big Bend National Park where we walked down to the banks of the Rio Grande, waved to the freelance guide on the other side who rowed over so we could hop into his boat for a quick tour of the little Mexican village on the other side. An interesting experience.

* Savoring café au lait and beignets at the outdoor tables of Café du Monde, New Orleans.

* Door County, WI at cherry blossom time. The lighthouse tour, fish fry (literally) and the rugged beauty of the Lake Michigan coastline.

* Camping on the beach of South Padre Island, Texas.

* San Antonio's Riverwalk at Christmas.

* Archway Monument in Nebraska. The only attraction ever built over an interstate as a tribute to America's pioneer spirit from covered wagons to RVs.

* Pasties in the Upper Peninsula of Michigan.

* Sunset Celebration in Key West, FL. It's held every night and, somehow, the event never gets old.

* Picking fruit at Capitol Reef National Park.

* Vast, sweeping corn fields rolling past the window as we go through farmland in Iowa, a pleasant ride periodically punctuated by the unmistakably pungent fragrance of the state's other major crop.

* The summertime enjoyment of riding the ski lift up Vail Mountain, CO and walking on snow at the top.

* Early Sunday morning services at the Grand Canyon chapel where there's a unique and charming wall mural.

* Headwaters of the Mississippi River where we were surprised to see the source of the mighty Mississippi as a mere pond.

* Valley of Fires in New Mexico, a little-known Bureau of Land Management recreation area with a fascinating history.

* Driving through fruit country in Central CA and stopping at a roadside stand to buy ultra-sweet, just-picked fruit.

* The high mountain experiences of Mt. Washington (NH) and Pike's Peak (CO).

* The panorama of America's heartland, neat, orderly farms, tiny towns and little coffee shops where the locals hang out.

* The unexpected lovely outdoor art in small towns: bright painted horses standing on street corners in Ocala, FL, colorful fish in Sturgeon Bay, WI, artistic kiddie cars in Elmhurst, IL….murals on many buildings depicting: frogs in Rayne, LA, Old West events in Toppenish, WA and Wizard of Oz scenes in Grand Rapids, WI.

* A picturesque crossing of Lake Powell, with our motor home piggy-backed on the back of the boat.

* Spectacular views from the co-pilot's seat during a southbound drive on the Pacific Coast Highway.

* The view from the many bridges we crossed back and forth over the Mighty Mississippi.

* Last but not least, the special places in Illinois, where I always leave a piece of my heart when I leave.

Glossary

Adapter — A device added to the RV power cord that enables the cord to secure a proper fit into a campground electric hookup outlet.

Aftermarket — The part of the RV industry that provides products and services available to RV owners following the initial RV purchase.

Age-Restricted Park — An RV park or resort specifically designated for people who are 55 and older.

Alternator — An engine-mounted device that produces 12-volt DC electricity for battery charging and other 12-volt functions while the engine is running.

Backup Monitoring System — A rear-mounted camera and a display screen in the cockpit designed to help the driver backing up large vehicles.

Big Rig — A nickname given to the pricey, modern and large (generally with multiple slideouts) Class A motor homes.

Black Water — Waste and water materials generally from the RV's toilet.

Black Water Holding Tank — The tank where the black water is flushed and held until emptied (dumped) later.

Blacktop Boondocking — Free overnight parking without any electric, water or sewer connections in a paved parking area with the property owner's permission. Often called dry camping.

Boondocking — Camping without any electric, water or sewer connections, generally out in the boonies (remote wooded areas) and without paying a camping fee.

Break-Away Switch — A switch that automatically applies the breaks on a vehicle that's being towed should that vehicle break loose from the vehicle that's towing it.

Breaking Camp — All the procedures involved in unhooking and preparing to leave the campsite.

Cab — The cockpit or driver's area of the RV.

Camper Van — A Class B motorized RV.

Campground — An area that has campsites (with hookups) for rent; also has a bath house with showers and toilets.

Campsite — The fee-pay piece of land in a campground that RVs rent. The site generally has electric and water hookups; often – but not always – a sewer hookup is at each site.

Campground Host — A person or couple who is employed by a campground to perform designated duties in return for a rent-free campsite and/or a salary.

Caravan — A group of RVs traveling together, generally with a wagonmaster guide.

Central Dump — A centralized area where an RV can pull up alongside a sewer hookup where black and grey water tanks can be emptied.

Class A Motor Home — A motorized RV built on a specially-designed chassis; can be gas or diesel-powered and provides driving and living areas all in one.

Class B Motor Home — A van camper, typically between 16 and 21 feet, that provides driving and living areas in a single vehicle.

Class C Motor Home — Commonly referred to as the mini-motor home. Built on a van frame, its most distinguishing feature.

Clearance — The distance between a vehicle's exterior height and potential obstructions such as bridges and overpasses.

Converter — A device that transforms 120-volt AC into usable 12-volt DC electricity for use on board an RV.

COW — Condo On Wheels. Luxurious big rigs are often called COWs.

Diesel Pusher — A motorhome powered by a rear-mounted diesel engine, equipped to propel rather than pull larger vehicles. Pushers are usually motorhomes over 34 feet in length.

Dolly — A two-wheeled trailer designed to tow a car with either its front wheels or its back wheels up off the ground.

Dinghy — An auxiliary vehicle being towed behind a motorized RV.

Dry Camping — Camping without any hookups; usually only done with self-contained RVs.

Dump Station — (See central dump.) An area that has a sewer opening where black and grey water tanks can be emptied.

Dump the Tanks — Procedure of emptying the black and grey water tanks.

Electric Hookup — Connection available at a campsite where the electric cord from the RV is plugged into an outside 120-volt electrical outlet to provide power inside the RV.

Engine Power — 12 volt DC power generated from the RV's or tow vehicle's engine.

Fifth Wheel — Unique type of trailer built to be towed by a pickup truck with a special hitch mounted in the bed of the pickup. It is the largest of the towables.

5er — Nickname for a fifth wheel trailer.

Folding Camper Trailer — Smallest of the towable RVs, it is often called a pop-up. On the road it looks like a small, shallow box; upon arrival at a camp site, it expands up and out to become a tent-type unit on a flat bed.

Four-Down Toad — An auxiliary vehicle being towed behind a motor home with all four wheels down.

Fresh Water Hookup — Connection made from the RV to an outside fresh water source, available at most campsites.

Fresh Water Storage Tank — Tank under the RV where fresh water is stored ready for use.

Fresh Water System — Clean running water system within the RV for all faucets, sinks, shower, water heater and to maintain the water level in the toilet.

Full-Timers — People who live and travel in an RV year-round; sometimes called "365ers."

Full Hookup — A campsite that has water, electric and sewer hookups directly at the site. Often referred to as "3-point" hookup.

Generator — A device driven by an internal combustion engine that produces 120-volt electricity to be used in the RV when other sources of electricity are not available.

Gooseneck — The part of the fifth wheel trailer that fits into the bed of the pickup truck to make a connection for towing.

Grey Water — Used water from the RV sinks, tub and shower.

Grey Water Holding Tank — Tanks where the grey water is held until it is emptied (dumped).

Gross Combined Vehicle Weight Rating (GCVW) — The maximum weight limit for a tow vehicle, object or vehicle being towed and all passengers, cargo and liquid inside.

Hitch — The device that provides a connection between the tow vehicle and the vehicle being towed. There are various classes of hitches depending on the weight they are designed to pull.

Hookups — Outside utilities that are made available for an RV to use; these include electric, water, sewer, cable TV and phone.

Jacks — Stabilizing apparatus that are manually or electronically lowered to level and stabilize an RV after it is parked at its campsite.

Kingpin — The part of a fifth wheel trailer that slides and locks into the hitch that is mounted in the bed of the pickup truck tow vehicle.

Leveling Bar — Part of the hitch designed to properly disperse the weight among the axles.

LP Gas — Propane that fuels many of the appliances on board the RV.

Making Camp — All the procedures involved in pulling in, hooking up and preparing for a stay at the campsite.

Mini-Motor Home — See Class C Motor Home.

Monitor Panel — A display unit inside the RV that provides information about the on board systems including levels of the tanks and voltage being used in the electrical system.

Motor Home — See Class A Motor Home.

No-Toad — Nickname for the Class B van campers because they generally do not tow a dinghy.

Pop-Up — Smallest of the towable RVs, also called a Folding Camper Trailer. On the road it looks like a small, shallow box; upon arrival at a camp site, it expands up and out to become a tent-type unit on a flat bed.

Propane — See LP gas.

Pull-Through Site — A campsite with access from either end, allowing the RV to pull directly into the site, thus eliminating the need to back into the site.

Pusher — See diesel pusher.

Rally — A large get-together of RVers, often sponsored by a camping club or organization.

Recreational Vehicle (RV) — A home-on-wheels that provides the convenience of travel and living quarters all in the same vehicle.

Rig — A nickname used to refer to the entire RV unit, either tow vehicle and trailer or motor home and toad.

RV Dinosaur — Nickname for RVs that are more than 20 years old.

RV Newbies — People who are new to the RV lifestyle.

RV Park — A campground that is more modern, generally featuring longer, wider sites to accommodate newer rigs.

RV Resort — An RV park with larger sites and amenities such as pool, spa, golf, tennis, etc.

RV Show — A venue for displaying the latest recreational vehicles and products and in the same location.

RV Wannabies — People who have never gone RVing but who are planning to become RVers in the future.

Safety Chains — Additional towing attachment that prevents a towed vehicle from veering off in case of separation during transit.

Sewer Connection — Connection at a campsite that allows the black and grey water tanks to be emptied right at the site.

Site — Short for campsite.

Slideout — Sections of the RV's interior that expand outward several feet after the RV is parked. The slideouts widen the inside rooms and create more space on board.

Snow Bird — RVers who spend the winter season in warmer climates and return north during warm weather months.

Snow Bird Park — RV park or resort that caters to retirees who spend the winter season in sun-belt states.

Sport Utility Trailer — Sometimes called "toy haulers," this specially designed trailer has living quarters plus a garage at the back to store cycles, ATVs and other sports vehicles or equipment.

Stick-Built House — Any house or home not on wheels; a site-built home.

Surge Protector — A device attached between an incoming electrical power source and the RV designed to intercept any power surges or spikes that could harm RV wiring and appliances.

Sway Control Bar — An accessory device designed to stabilize and restrict motion between a tow vehicle and the vehicle being towed.

Toad — A dinghy or auxiliary vehicle being towed behind a motor home.

Tow Bar — A device used for towing a dinghy behind a motor home.

Tow Rating — The maximum weight a vehicle can safely tow.

Tow Vehicle — The vehicle responsible for towing another vehicle.

Towable — An RV that relies on another vehicle to tow it.

Travel Trailer — The most common towable RV. Its sub-class is a lightweight travel trailer.

Truck Camper — A camper attached to the bed of a pickup truck.

Van Camper — See Class B Motor Home.

Walk-Around — Final check of the RV prior to leaving a campsite or boondocking spot. Walk-around routine includes checking the interior and exterior of the vehicle(s) and check of the surrounding area.

Water Pump — Device designed to force water from the fresh water tank through the pipes on board the RV.

Wagonmaster — An individual who is responsible for leading an RV caravan.

Workamper — A general term that refers to people who work at campgrounds as well as campers/travelers who work during the course of their travels.

Did you know...

The world's oldest Winnebago and the smallest Airstream in the world are among the exhibits at the 100,000 square-foot Recreational Vehicle/Motor Home Hall of Fame located in Elkhart, Indiana.

Index of Online Resources

"A little learning is a dangerous thing."
—*Alexander Pope*

"Knowledge is power."
—*Sir Francis Bacon*

Scattered throughout the book are "online resources" for various aspects of RVing and the RV lifestyle. This section lists all of them alphabetically by category.

IMPORTANT NOTE: Resources referenced in this book are meant to be suggestive only. In most cases the information you glean from a particular source should add to other research on that topic. Never rely on one individual or on a single website for information on RVing topics and issues, or to make important decisions.

Blacktop Boondocking

www.overnightrvparking.com
Over 11,000 locations, U.S. & Canada; Facebook & mobile devices, too.

www.travelbooksusa.com

Casino Camping lists hundreds of RV-friendly locations. State-by-state locator maps.

Walmart Atlas lists over 4,000 Walmarts & Sam's Club locations; identifies fuel availability.

Campgrounds & RV Parks

www.campingroadtrip.com
18,000 campgrounds, RV parks & RV resorts on *Camp Finder* app (iPhone & Android). Free access to the list on website.

www.koa.com
Over 400 Campgrounds in the network. Free directory; locator maps on website. Smartphone app available.

www.goodsamcamping.com
North American Camping Guide includes 13,500 listings. Good Sam apps available.

www.gocampingamerica.com/search
Search for campgrounds/RV parks by city, state or landmark name.

www.rvparkreviews.com
User-submitted reviews by campers of facilities throughout the U.S.

www.freecampgrounds.com
Free and inexpensive (under $10) camping places. Click on a map for detailed listings by state.

www.freecampsites.net
Community-driven platform for free camping locations.

Camping on Public Lands

www.recreation.gov
Online reservations for camping at facilities managed by National Park Service, Forest Service, Army Corps of Engineers, Bureau of Land Management, Bureau of Reclamation and U.S. Fish & Wildlife Service.

www.travelbooksusa.com
Corps Camping & *National Park Service Camping Guide* are books that identify areas with sites for RVs.

www.nps.gov/findapark/passes.htm
Information on the *America the Beautiful* passes.

Caravans & Tours

www.fantasyrvtours.com
Guided RV vacations around the world.

www.rvalaskatours.com
RV tours to Alaska.

www.adventurecaravans.com
Guided tours in the United States, Canada and Mexico.

www.yankeetours.com
Unique escorted package tours in the U.S. and Canada.

Checklists

www.rv-roadtrips.thefuntimesguide.com/checklists/
Good advice plus links to effective checklists to use as models.

www.changingears.com/rv-sec-checklists/
Printable arrival and setup checklists for trailers and motor homes.

Android and iPhone apps
RV Checklist app; free for Android; $.99 for iPhone

Clubs & Online Forum Communities

www.goodsamclub.com
Good Sam Club, the nation's largest camping club; state & local chapters; large national rallies.

www.rv.net
Open Roads Forum, largest RV forum. Affiliated with Good Sam Club, Woodall's, Trailer Life & Motor Home publications.

www.fmca.com
Family Motor Coach Association for motor home owners. Lots of manufacturer-specific clubs. Active Forum. Regional & international rallies.

www.escapees.com
Escapees Club founded as a support and service network for full-timers. Sponsors a good Boot Camp for newbies. Large membership & open to all RVers.

www.rvnetwork.com
Forum sponsored by Escapees, high participation by experienced, knowledgeable RVers.

www.iRV2.com
Leading online forum community; diverse forums, many for special interests; sponsors and promotes rallies.

www.rvforum.net
Oldest rv-related online community. Promotes mini rallies. Forum popular with retirees.

www.rv-dreams.com/forum
Friendly forum to collect and share information. Sponsors rallies.

Clubs: Camping Membership

www.camphalfprice.com
Happy Camper Club, nearly 1,200 campgrounds, half off for members. Find locations online or in the directory. Low annual dues.

www.passportamerica.com
Passport America, 50% off camping with membership card. Over 1,800 campgrounds. App available for Android & Apple; locator map on the website. Low membership fee. Organization sponsors annual Fun Rally.

www.thousandtrails.com
Campground membership organization with 80 parks; purchase annual pass.

www.coastresorts.com
Coast to Coast membership camping network of RV resorts & campgrounds; annual membership contract.

www.membershipresale.com
Specializing in resale of major campground membership contracts.

Clubs: Special Interest

www.rvingwomen.com
National network with chapters throughout the U.S. Rallies & educational events.

www.lonersonwheels.com
Club for single campers & travelers; not a matchmaking or dating service.

www.naarva.com
National African-American RV Association.

www.gonct.com
National Camping Travelers, a Masonic family camping club.

www.fcrv.org
Family Campers & RVers, dedicated to camping fellowship. Local chapters, monthly campouts, annual Campvention.

www.explorer-rvclub.com
Canada's largest RV club.

Dump Stations

www.rvdumps.com
Find RV dump stations throughout the country.

www.sanidumps.com
Lists dump stations in the U.S. and Canada.

Education

www.rveducation101.com
RV training videos and DVDs.

For Sale: New & Used RVs

www.rvusa.com
RV Marketplace for buyers, sellers and owners.

www.rvonline.com
Features new and used RV's for sale.

www.rvtrader.com
Large inventory; multiple search options.

Global Positioning Systems (GPS)

www.randmcnally.com
First company to develop RV-specific receiver, RVND. 7-inch screen.

www.garmin.com
Garmin RV GPS. 7-inch screen.

www.magellen.com
Magellen RoadMate for RV. 5-inch screen.

Insurance

www.explorerrv.com
Specializes in insurance for RVs.

www.rvainsurance.com
RV America offers comparative insurance quotes.

Mail Service

www.usps.gov
For snow birds: use "change of address" to get mail sent to temporary location & vice versa. Use "hold mail" if you'll be away less than 30 days.

www.escapees.com/mailforwardingservice/howtoapply.asp
Mail forwarding service founded by full-time RVers.

www.fmca.com
Mail forwarding service from Family Motor Coach Association.

Maintenance

www.rveducation101.com
Comprehensive site with information about using and maintaining your RV.

www.rvdoctor.com
View articles about RV maintenance and safety. Post a technical question or read previous Q&A's.

www.doityourselfrv.com
Click on *Projects* tab for information on maintenance and repairs.

Manufacturers

www.rvia.org
Recreation Vehicle Industry Association, national trade association representing RV manufacturers and their component parts suppliers.

www.rversonline.com
The *Info Resources* page has links to major manufacturers.

Online Travel Newsletters

www.rvtravel.com
Free newsletters and daily tips covering RV and travel information.

www.wheellife.com
Timely information about RV lifestyle, people and destinations.

Prescription Drugs

www.cvs.com
Over 7,600 stores nationwide. Store locator feature on website.

www.walgreens.com
Over 8,000 stores nationwide. Store locator feature on website.

www.walmart.com
Over 4,000 stores nationwide. Store locator feature on website.

Road Service Plans

www.coachnet.com
Knowledgeable and timely emergency service specifically for RVs.

www.goodsamroadside.com
Emergency Roadside Service plan sponsored by Good Sam Club.

RV Driving School

www.rvschool.com
Learn how to drive or tow your RV from certified instructors. Training available at several locations across the U.S. Seminars offered all year.

RV Lifestyle

www.gorving.com
Comprehensive information about the RV lifestyle & activities; free newsletter.

www.doityourselfrv.com
RV enthusiasts share the best the Internet has to offer about the RV lifestyle & how to make the most of your RV. Click on the "Funny" tab for comic relief.

www.rversonline.org
Over 2,000 pages of non-commercial RV-related information based on the premise of RVers helping RVers. No advertising on this site. Also has a Facebook page.

RV Recall Information

www.recalls.gov
National Highway Safety Administration (NHTSA) database of all vehicle recalls (including RVs) listed by make, model & year.

RV Rentals

www.cruiseamerica.com
Largest RV rental company in the United States.

www.elmonterv.com
Based in California, has locations throughout the U.S.

RV Shows

www.rvia.org
Current calendar of RV shows throughout the U.S. and Canada.

www.thebestrvshow.com
California RV show, called the "granddaddy of shows," held every October.

www.chicagorvshow.com
Largest show in the Midwest.

Safety

www.rvsafety.org
Official site of the Recreation Vehicle Safety Education Foundation.

www.catscale.com
Find locations of CAT scales across the U.S.

www.changingears.com
Departure checklist for trailers in *RV Checklists* section.

Satellite Equipment

www.kvh.com
Mobile satellite dish systems for TV and Internet.

www.winegard.com
Satellite dish antennas, roof-mounted and portable with tripod.

www.kingcontrols.com
Satellite TV dish antennas and accessories.

Satellite Internet Provider

www.hughesnet.com
Provides full Internet access via satellite modem. Largest provider nationwide.

Satellite TV Providers

www.dish.com
Satellite TV provider - entertainment, sports, movies, many channels. Internet service also available.

www.directtv.com
Satellite TV provider - entertainment, sports, movies, many channels. Internet service also available.

Selecting A Home State

www.travelbooksusa.com
Choosing Your RV Home Base book to compare factors for selecting a home base. Also available at Amazon.com.

Smartphones & Internet Connections

www.att.com/wireless
Large nationwide carrier offering smartphones, service, support & Internet connection. Corporate and online stores.

www.verizon.com
Large nationwide carrier offering smartphones, service, support & Internet connection. Corporate and online stores.

Snow Bird Destinations

www.arizonaguide.com
Official website of the Arizona Office of Tourism.

www.visitcalifornia.com
California's official tourism website.

www.visitflorida.com
Florida's official tourism and travel planning website.

www.traveltex.com
The official Texas tourism website.

Supplies

www.campingworld.com
Supplies, equipment, RV accessories, service, etc.

www.rvupgrades.com
Specializes in unique RV accessories and supplies.

www.walmart.com/cp/RV-Accessories/1070265
RV accessories and supplies. Free store pickup.

Towing Guides

www.trailerlife.com
Publishes an annual Towing Guide; may be printed from the website.

www.motorhomemagazine.com
Publishes the annual Dinghy Towing Guide; available in PDF format.

Trip Planning

www.googlemaps.com
Free online trip planning tool. Pinpoints campground locations by state.

www.randmcnally.com
Publisher of the traditional Road Atlas.

www.campingroadtrip.com
Devoted to helping people plan road trips, includes campground listings and a forum.
Also developed "Camp Finder" app.

www.travelbooksusa.com
Unique selection of travel & RV books in online bookstore.

www.rvbookstore.com
Online bookstore dedicated to all things RV.

Used RV Prices

www.nadaguides.com
Click on *Recreation Vehicles* to get values for used RVs.

Vehicle License & Registration

www.dmv.org
Nationwide Departments of Motor Vehicles state-by-state guide.

www.usa.gov/Topics/Motor-Vehicles.shtml
Links for all 50 states to get or renew your driver's license, register your vehicle, or other motor vehicle services.

Work Opportunities

www.workamper.com
Brings job seekers and employers together.

www.work-camping.com
Work camping jobs at Recreation Resource Management.

www.camphost.org
Information about becoming a campground host at Recreation Resource Management areas.

www.nps.gov/personnel
This site is designed to provide basic information about job opportunities with the National Park Service.

www.fs.fed.us/fsjobs
Temporary employment opportunities with the U.S. Forest Service.

www.yellowstonejobs.com
Yellowstone National Park employment options.

www.workatkoa.com
Job opportunities at KOA campgrounds.

www.workersonwheels.com
Jobs and resources for full-timers, work campers and other RVers.

www.nps.gov/yose/jobs/
Yosemite National Park employment options.

CPSIA information can be obtained at www.ICGtesting.com
Printed in the USA
BVOW09s0221181215

430584BV00019B/685/P

9 781885 464521